SAN FRANCISCO'S
ST. CECILIA PARISH

SAN FRANCISCO'S
ST. CECILIA PARISH

· *A History* ·

FRANK DUNNIGAN

THE
History
PRESS

Published by The History Press
Charleston, SC
www.historypress.net

Panoramic front/back cover image is of St. Cecilia "Pioneers" posing in front of the original church/rectory at 1215 Taraval Street in 1927 on the occasion of the parish's tenth anniversary. *Parish Archives*.

First published 2016

Manufactured in the United States

ISBN 978.1.46713.604.4

Library of Congress Control Number: 2016944046

To my grandmother
Josephine Creem Dunnigan,

as well as to my parents,
Frank and Katherine Dunnigan,

St. Cecilia parishioners from 1937 until 2002

Original artwork by Staci Kavanagh, reproduced with her permission.

Remembering all those who have been a part of St. Cecilia Parish over the past one hundred years:

For where we have been,
For where we are today,
For where we are heading,
Let us give thanks to God.

Corner of 15th and Taraval, 1917, looking down 15th Avenue. Church construction was about to begin at far left. Note that cobblestones outline the eventual route of the Taraval streetcar and that concrete pillars have been installed to support future power lines for streetcar operations that began in February 1918. *Parish Archives.*

CONTENTS

FOREWORD

With joy and gratitude, we celebrate one hundred glorious and grace-filled years in the life of the St. Cecilia Parish family!

As we celebrate, we step back and admire with awe and pride a century of growth in faith, service to the needy, education for the youth and Christlike support for the suffering. All of this forms a magnificent mosaic depicting the incredible history of St. Cecilia Parish. The colorful mosaic portrays happy and joyful experiences—baptisms, first Holy Communions, graduations, weddings and anniversary celebrations. Then there is the outpouring of charity for the needy and less fortunate. We also see pictured loving support for the sick, the suffering and the dying. Finally, we observe the prayerful remembrance of our deceased relatives and friends. What a marvelous picture of ten decades of bringing Jesus Christ and his church to the Parkside District of San Francisco! Every one of the numerous pieces making up our mosaic represents each one of the thousands of parishioners who have shared in our parish history.

We devoutly express our profound gratitude to the dedicated pastors, associates, Sisters and generous parishioners who have provided this spiritual care and loving support for ten decades.

As we stand back, admiring this glorious centennial mosaic, we offer our heartfelt prayers and gratitude for the countless blessings showered on our parish. We ask Our Blessed Lord to continue to bestow these same blessings on all who will be part of our parish family for the next one hundred years and who will add their own special pieces to the St. Cecilia family mosaic.

Joanne Olivieri photo.

The author is deeply indebted to current pastor Monsignor Michael D. Harriman and also to Monsignor James P. McKay, parish priest from 1956 to 1962 and pastor from 1976 to 1990, for their invaluable assistance in commemorating the many details of community life during their combined forty-plus years of service among the St. Cecilia Parish family.

ACKNOWLEDGEMENTS

Many individuals, both living and deceased, along with several organizations have contributed to the history, photos and reminiscences included in this book. The author is indebted to each and every one of them for their contributions.

Mary Ahlbach
Tom and Nicole Angsten
Archdiocesan Archives–San Francisco
Archives—Sisters of the Holy Names
Ann Basuino
Sue Bunnell
Sarah Cantor
Fran Cavanagh
Anne Bosque Collins
Monsignor Harold E. Collins
Marian Connelly
Jerian Reidy Crosby
Rosie Dominguez
Joan Donohue
Robert Drucker
Dr. Renee Duffey
Virginia Fabi
Sister Michaeline Falvey, SNJM

Eric Fischer
Abigail Fleming
Darin Fong
Claire Mibach Fugate
David Gallagher
Randa Ghnaim
Vivian Gisin
Eric Godtland
Lynn Goldfinger-Abram
Veronica Granucci
Grieg family
Doris Grimley
Yanli and Jorge Guerzon
Paul Haettenschwiller
Annette Hagan
Father Thomas Hamilton
Monsignor Michael D. Harriman
Harrington family

ACKNOWLEDGEMENTS

Rene Herrerias
Carolyn Hewes
Bernadette Hooper
Rosie Horan
Robert Hurrell
Mike Huynh
Eugene Ide
Barbara Smith Johnson
Delphine Strehl Johnson
Paul Judge
Staci Kavanagh
Kathy Kays
Chris Keller
Dolores Bosque Kelly-Hons
Thomas Kennedy
Rio Kim
Sister Margaret Kinzie, SNJM
Woody LaBounty
Megan Laddusaw
Mary Landers
Jacqueline Lane
Charley Lavery
John and Marilyn Lee
Luana Letele
Betty Lew
Lynch family
Nancy Mazza
Maureen McCarthy
Will McCullar
Andreliz Bautista McGlade
Terry McHugh
Monsignor James P. McKay
McKeon family
Meagher family
Mibach family
Sister Marilyn Miller, SNJM

Cathy Moura
Sally Mulkerrins
Phil and Helen Murphy
Peggy O'Brien
Joanne Olivieri
Sister Kathryn Ondreyco, SNJM
Tom O'Toole
Kathleen Dougherty Overbey
Paulsen family
Anne Phipps
Patricia Pinnick
Jo Anne Quinn
Tony and Cathy Ribera
Catherine Ring
John Ring
Mary Ellen (MER) Ring
Paul Rosenberg
Bernadette Ruane
Christine Ruck
Cathy Smith Saffel
San Francisco Public Library
Mary Scanlon
Marina Simonian
Roger Smith
Father Patrick Summerhays
Donald Thieler
Lorri Ungaretti
Dennis Urbiztondo
Christine Vega
Nano K. Visser
Fred Walsh
Teri Watters
John and Linda Westerhouse
Ray Williamson
Kitty Wolfinger
Craig Wolfrom

And to all the members of the Centennial Committee!

INTRODUCTION

My own family joined St. Cecilia Parish when my fifty-seven-year-old widowed grandmother, Josephine Dunnigan, along with her two college-age sons (my father and his brother), moved to 21st Avenue and Rivera Street in 1937. Grandma remained a faithful attendee at the 12:15 p.m. Sunday Mass until her passing in 1960 at age eighty.

In the late 1940s, my parents were married and soon bought their first and only home on 18th Avenue near Vicente Street. It was from there that I received the sacraments of baptism, confession, First Communion and confirmation before finishing St. Cecilia School and going on to graduate from St. Ignatius and the University of San Francisco.

Like his mother, Dad remained in St. Cecilia's parish for the remainder of his life, until we held his funeral on a typically foggy July day in 1980 (my uncle and his wife also made that final visit down the middle aisle of St. Cecilia Church in 1988 and 1965, respectively). Mom remained an active parishioner for another twenty-two years, living independently at home and receiving weekly visits and Holy Communion from Father Duquet in her last few years, until her passing in 2002 when she was nearly ninety.

Since 2008, I have been writing a monthly column on neighborhood history, and in 2014, The History Press published a compilation of those recollections and other historical reminiscences, plus a sequel two years later. Now it's time to explore, in some depth, that corner of the Parkside District that is St. Cecilia Parish—the formation and early years, its growth and development after World War II and the changes that have been evolving over the last quarter century or more. Most of all, I want to share the personal stories of some of the thousands of people who have formed the St. Cecilia Parish family over the past one hundred years.

In the course of researching this book, I have spent many days and nights working in the rectory. It was on one of my early visits in 2015 that I noticed a framed photo of Monsignor Harold Collins—the longest-serving pastor, from 1946 to 1976—hanging in the narrow hallway between the front entry and the parlor. Many people have commented that "the old man continues to keep an eye on things around here." From the time that he went to be with the Lord in December 1980, most of what he has witnessed has surely pleased him greatly, although there have undoubtedly been some troubling moments. Through the years, it is clear that all of us associated with the parish—then and now— remain beneficiaries of his good works in so many different ways.

Now, sit back and enjoy the view as we take a nostalgic ride back through the last ten decades of life in San Francisco's St. Cecilia Parish—"the Finest, the Greatest and the Best."

Chapter 1

IN THE BEGINNING

Pre-1917

The story of San Francisco and its rise from a dusty outpost of civilization to a major city of the world is inextricably intertwined with the story of the Catholic Church in the United States.

From the founding of Mission Dolores in 1776 until the post–World War II era, San Francisco's large Catholic population defined the course of city history. From a largely agrarian population and then to a blue-collar labor force, the economic situation of the population gradually improved as many Catholics moved into business, local government, law enforcement and the professions. The Roman Catholic population remained dominant in the forty-nine-square-mile city of San Francisco for decades. It is anecdotal, but completely true, that for many years, the archbishop of San Francisco was consulted prior to the appointment of any police or fire chief in the city.

It was during the early years of this Catholic-dominant period of city history that St. Cecilia Parish came into being. The Sunset District, with rolling sand dunes and freshwater ponds, was originally home to a variety of wildlife, plus colorful flora and fauna that changed with the seasons. All of that began to fade shortly after the Mid-Winter Fair of 1894 was held in Golden Gate Park, not far from the present-day intersection of 9th Avenue and Lincoln Way.

Before long, San Franciscans seeking to escape from the noise and pollution of the crowded neighborhoods closer to downtown sought to build homes in the area just south of the fair site. Within a few years, the population grew, and St. Anne of the Sunset Parish was formed in

1904 with sweeping boundaries—from Twin Peaks all the way to the Pacific Ocean.

The original church of St. Anne Parish, built in 1905, was destroyed in the 1906 earthquake, and a new temporary structure was then built facing Funston Avenue—twenty-five years prior to construction of the present St. Anne Church on Judah Street. The little parish in the sand dunes continued growing, as many newcomers were arriving daily, seeking new homes to replace those lost in the earthquake and fire of 1906.

By 1909, San Francisco had largely rebuilt itself from the devastation of just three years earlier. The local economy was booming, there was very low unemployment and skilled workers were being recruited from all over the country because of a shortage of laborers here. Things were looking up for the City by the Golden Gate.

Throughout the rest of the world, however, things were changing in those early years of the twentieth century. In Europe, old monarchies were being swept aside as the world war raged on from its beginnings in the summer of 1914. In the spring of 1916, there was an uprising in Ireland against British rule, and Russia was soon on the brink of a revolution that would topple its czarist regime. In nearby Mexico, the revolution that began in 1910 was still ongoing. Social, political and economic unrest seemed to encompass the entire globe.

Father John P. Tobin (1876–1929), first pastor of St. Cecilia Church, 1917–29. *Parish Archives.*

It was against this world backdrop that, late in 1916, San Francisco archbishop Edward Joseph Hanna determined that another Catholic parish was needed in the western part of San Francisco in order to relieve the overcrowded conditions at St. Anne Church.

On January 7, 1917, St. Cecilia Parish was formed by partitioning off the southern portion of St. Anne Parish. The newly appointed St. Cecilia pastor, Father John P. Tobin, a native of Ireland, celebrated the first Mass in the history of the new parish in the dining room of a converted two-story house at 1215 Taraval Street. That structure also included his living quarters, and the building, still standing today—though greatly modified—soon became known as St. Cecilia's Parish House. A new era in the history of San Francisco was suddenly born.

Meanwhile, the United States was less than ninety days away from entering that fateful conflict known as World War I.

Chapter 2

THE EARLY DAYS

1917–1929

Almost immediately after the parish was established, Father Tobin realized that the small house at 1215 Taraval was in no way adequate to provide for the long-term needs of the fifty-nine Catholic families residing within the boundaries of the new parish. Work immediately began on building a larger church a few blocks away to accommodate the burgeoning population of the neighborhood.

Within the first two months, Father Tobin was successful in acquiring an old school building from the City and County of San Francisco. The tiny, two-room wooden structure known as Parkside School had been located at 31st Avenue and Taraval Street. Donated by Mayor James ("Sunny Jim") Rolph to St. Cecilia Parish, the rather dilapidated building was then moved to a recently purchased lot at 15th and Taraval Street and was in place by Holy Thursday, April 5, 1917—a date that historians will note was just twenty-four hours before the U.S. Congress voted to enter World War I. These were perilous times, indeed.

Remodeling then began, often with Father Tobin donning overalls, picking up a handsaw and participating in the work himself. Just a few months later, on a Sunday morning in the early summer of 1917, the new St. Cecilia Church was dedicated by Archbishop Edward J. Hanna before a crowd of hundreds of jubilant parishioners. For a cost of under $14,000, St. Cecilia Parish had acquired a choice lot and built a new church for the community. The dream had been achieved.

Originally partitioned off from the St. Anne parish in 1917, St. Cecilia Parish extended from Twin Peaks to the Pacific Ocean and from Pacheco Street on the north to Sloat Boulevard on the south. From only fifty-nine families in 1917, the parish grew to well over four hundred families in that first decade.

The city-owned Twin Peaks Tunnel, linking the vast western neighborhoods of San Francisco to the downtown business district, was completed in 1917, the same year that St. Cecilia Parish was founded, and revenue service began early in the new year of 1918. Suddenly, thousands of San Franciscans began to think seriously about moving to the west of Twin Peaks, with the guarantee of efficient and inexpensive transit to the central part of the city, where many people were employed. The once empty sand dunes began to sprout new homes and businesses overnight, and the new parish began to grow rapidly.

Dedication of St. Cecilia Church, 1917. Unlike some later images that show a slightly smaller crowd, this is the actual day of the church dedication. Note that scaffolding is still hanging from the steeple, light fixtures are not yet installed above the entrance and unfinished painting and roof work remain to be completed. No streetcar tracks appear in this image, as they do in later photos, since the tracks were not installed until just a few months prior to the start of revenue service in February 1918. Some of the houses in the distance, on 19th and 20th Avenues, between Taraval and Ulloa, remain today. *Wolfinger family photo, courtesy of Barbara Smith Johnson.*

PERSONAL REMINISCENCE: KITTY WOLFINGER (1887–1979)

I was born in the Mission District, but when we married, my husband and I wanted to raise our children in the fresh air, away from all the noise and traffic of the Mission. We first settled into a house on 23rd Avenue near Vicente Street and later moved to a larger home on 20th Avenue near Larsen Park. My husband and I, along with our children, were one of the original fifty-nine families that made up St. Cecilia Parish when it was formed in 1917. The parish did not have an elementary school in those days, so my children had to go elsewhere, but they did go to Catholic high schools. The 15th Avenue and Taraval location for the church was there even before the L-line streetcars began running. We were very happy when the church moved downhill to 17th Avenue in 1928, as it made for a much easier walk on Sunday mornings. I lost my husband in 1932 when I was just forty-five years old and our children were still high school and college age, but we all remained together in our family home until they became older. My daughter was the last one to marry, in 1940, and she was reluctant to leave me alone in such a big house, so she and her husband moved in with me following their wedding and raised their five children in our family home—with my grandchildren all attending St. Cecilia School from the early 1940s until the last one graduated in 1966. I was personally acquainted with Pastors Tobin, Harnett, Collins and McKay—and all of them were wonderful priests who were devoted to the members of this parish.

Author's note: Members of Mrs. Wolfinger's large family owned and lived in her old home until early in this new millennium—still St. Cecilia parishioners. Her descendants include three children, nine grandchildren, eighteen great-grandchildren, thirty great-great-grandchildren and at least one great-great-great-grandchild—all of whom live beyond San Francisco today yet share a fondness for the stories of the early days of St. Cecilia Parish.

With the new church at 15th Avenue and Taraval Street completed in 1917, Father Tobin purchased in 1920 for $8,500 a newly constructed building at 608 Taraval Street, just a block away, between 16th and 17th Avenues, to serve as a rectory, with a large hall in the garage for the growing number of parish groups and organizations. By purchasing a new rectory closer to the church, Father Tobin and the other assigned priests

Looking east on Taraval, 1920. The new rectory is at left, with 16th Avenue intersecting Taraval between the rectory and the church, located at 15th and Taraval in the distance. The new parish hall would soon be built at the northeast corner of 16th and Taraval, between these two structures. *Parish Archives.*

were spared the six-block uphill walk along a foggy Taraval Street (with many unpaved sidewalks) from the original St. Cecilia's Parish House at 1215 Taraval, just west of 22nd Avenue, when it was time to say Mass. The church building at 15th and Taraval was enlarged and remodeled that same year, just three years after its dedication, yet the conditions at Sunday Mass remained seriously overcrowded.

In 1923, a new parish hall was built at the northeast corner of 16th and Taraval, just west of the church building and half a block from the new rectory, for a cost of under $10,000. This building, too, was actively used and would remain an integral part of parish life for the next thirty-three years. The following year, 1924, saw a further eighty-six-seat expansion of the 15th and Taraval church building, at a cost of $2,000, although by now it was widely regarded that the 1917 church structure would ultimately have to be replaced with something larger.

By 1927, Father Tobin, then in his role as pastor for just over ten years, met with his "consultors"—an advisory committee of twenty-four parishioners—and that group's ultimate recommendation was that a new church building was needed at once. The parish had grown tenfold in its first decade—from 59 families to 587. The decision was made to abandon the old schoolhouse-church and also to move and expand the parish hall from 16th and Taraval to a new lot that had been purchased on 17th Avenue, just south of Ulloa Street—with the idea that a permanent expansion of parish facilities, including a future school, would best be located away from a busy commercial street such as Taraval.

Although the price seems incredibly low today, the $65,000 cost for the nearly two-acre parcel between 17th and 18th Avenues, Ulloa and Vicente Streets, was a serious undertaking for a parish that had never spent that much money before on a single transaction. Landowner Carl Larsen (who also donated the 19th Avenue parcels now named Larsen Park to the city for recreational purposes) gave St. Cecilia Parish an excellent price for the new land. Father Tobin and his consultors had a vision for the future of the parish.

The relocation and expansion of the 1923 parish hall into a new 17th Avenue church in 1928 served the community well for nearly three full decades. The move also proved fortunate because of the terrain of the land on 17th Avenue. With street-level access to the church from 17th Avenue, the sloping land provided for a full-height "basement" hall beneath the church, with natural daylight and level access from the rear portion of the lot. The remodeled structure, blessed by Archbishop Hanna on June 19, 1928 (just eleven years after the founding of the parish), had a seating capacity of 732 persons—far larger than the expanded old church building—plus open meeting space below for all the parish organizations.

With the move of the church building to 17th Avenue, plans were made for an entire parish facility at that location, including a school, a convent for nuns, a permanent rectory and, someday, a much larger permanent church building. Father Tobin also relocated the rectory from 608 Taraval Street by purchasing a home at 2562 17th Avenue, directly across the street from the new church location, for $10,000. This building, too, would serve the parish for many years.

Before the start of the Great Depression in October 1929, residential building was booming in the entire western half of San Francisco, and even the new 17th Avenue church was often filled to capacity and then some. In response to this growth, the Archdiocese of San Francisco formed a new parish, St. Brendan (the same name as an older South-of-Market parish that was closed after 1906). The formation of this new parish from the northeast corner of St. Cecilia Parish in 1929 further relieved the overcrowding that was still present in the new facilities on 17th Avenue.

Sadly, Father John Tobin, founding pastor of St. Cecilia Parish, was not able to enjoy the newly completed St. Cecilia buildings for very long. He was taken home to be with the Lord early on Good Friday morning in 1929, when he was only in his early fifties, noted in the parish's Golden Jubilee book of 1967 as being "an older age then than it is today." Lacking the benefits of modern medicine, those people reaching their fifties at that time were presumed to have already lived "a rich, full life."

PERSONAL REMINISCENCE: ANNE BOSQUE COLLINS

My parents moved to St. Cecilia Parish in 1924 with a two-year-old son. Between that time and 1933, they had seven more children—a total of six boys and two girls—and they soon moved to a larger home on 15th Avenue near Taraval. Mother was a firm believer in education, and all of us attended St. Cecilia School before going on to Catholic high schools, and then all of us received college degrees—and our parents never complained about the cost. As we each married and had children of our own, our parents were blessed with more than forty grandchildren. When she died in 1967, just before her seventy-fifth birthday, Mother had been living in Novato for several years, but we still returned to St. Cecilia Church for her funeral—it was still "her parish" after all that time.

News accounts from the time tell us that Father Tobin had suffered from diabetes for several years but that his death was believed to have been caused by a heart attack. His funeral was one of the largest ever held in San Francisco, and the procession from the 17th Avenue church to Holy Cross Cemetery was so large that all traffic on 19th Avenue had to be stopped. Civic dignitaries were present in large numbers, and the Requiem Mass was offered by Archbishop Hanna.

The following article, by George Raine, appeared in *Catholic San Francisco* in May 2012, and it epitomizes the life of Father Tobin and his work here on earth. In addition to the people of St. Cecilia Parish, it is clear that the good father was also concerned with the less fortunate in our community (the article is reprinted here with the newspaper's express permission):

In a Burial Field without Headstones, a Pastor Lies
with His "Dear Friends"

Leafing through the interment record of Section A at Holy Cross Cemetery, the large, gently sloping burial ground that long ago was set aside for indigent persons, you'll notice that quite a few were laid to rest in the Great Depression years, when many people lost everything.

Section A, a field of 140,304 square feet at the northeast corner of Holy Cross, has room for 5,688 burials, but not all the allotted spaces are occupied. For many years Section A was exclusively the area used for burial of indigent people, but since the 1960s or 1970s the thinking at the

Father Tobin and four ladies of the parish standing on the steps of the 15th and Taraval church building in the World War I era. Note the small scale of the building, which seated only about 250 people at the time. *Parish Archives.*

cemetery—led by Roger Appleby, the recently retired general manager—has evolved to this: Indigent persons should be buried alongside everyone else, they should not be isolated.

"It is a continuation of the tradition that we take care of everyone," said Williams. "It is perhaps more reflective of an idea that we don't label people and that we don't separate people in the community as made up of people of various means and financial status," she said.

Most often, Holy Cross is contacted by the public administrator or the public guardian of San Francisco or San Mateo County—and sometimes a coroner's office, if the remains have been abandoned—for the burial of someone indigent. The cemetery also coordinates with the Missionaries of Charity who run a hospice in Pacifica for homeless men, some of whom have AIDS. For many years Holy Cross worked closely with the San Francisco College of Mortuary Science, now closed, which helped arrange burials.

There are no headstones in Section A. It is a pretty field, studded with English daisies. There is, however, near the center, a marble statute. It was dedicated by the St. Vincent de Paul Society and bears the name of Father John P. Tobin (1876–1929), the first pastor of St. Cecilia Parish in San Francisco, who is buried in front of it. Father Tobin wished to be buried with the needy people he had served at what was then called Laguna Honda Home in San Francisco—people he referred to as "my dear friends."

Father Tobin, born in Ireland, was an assistant pastor at Mission Dolores for 14 years before being assigned to St. Cecilia, in the sand dunes of the Parkside District, in 1917. He distinguished himself in part by acquiring property for a parish plant and launching St. Cecilia, but also by performing the corporal and spiritual works of mercy—just as the cemetery does, by burying the dead—among the poor of San Francisco.

He wanted to erect a statue, Williams said, that would memorialize the people who were buried in Section A. "He was very active in making sure that the poor of the City and County of San Francisco had a dignified Christian burial, so he had the statute erected," she said.

It bears the words of John 11:25: "I am the resurrection and the life; whoever believes in me, even if he dies, will live."

In his will, Father Tobin asked that the poor he had ministered to be taken care of in his absence. This included maintaining a ledger on which he tracked the very small amount of savings that some of the people had to their names. He left instructions on where the ledger was kept and asked that the accounting work continue.

That was his wish, along with being buried in what many people called Potter's Field—a term, also from Matthew, referring to ground not suited for agriculture, but more for the source of potter's clay—"a burying place for strangers."

It is entirely fitting that Father Tobin is remembered today not only for creating the vibrant parish life that so many of us have experienced during our time in the St. Cecilia community but also for his compassionate work with our less fortunate sisters and brothers.

Chapter 3

THE EXPANSION YEARS

1929–1946

In June 1929, Archbishop Hanna appointed Father John Harnett as the second pastor of St. Cecilia Parish. Father Harnett, another native of Ireland, born in 1873 and ordained a priest in 1897, arrived at St. Cecilia Parish in June 1929, just a few months before the stock market crash and the beginning of the Great Depression in October of that year.

The western neighborhoods of San Francisco were continuing to grow rapidly in the years after the conclusion of World War I. A second railway tunnel under the hills (the Duboce or Sunset Tunnel) had just opened in 1928, thus ensuring that more and more people would be settling west of Twin Peaks in the coming years.

Upon his arrival, Father Harnett took note of the plans established by his predecessor and group of consultors for the completion of a full parish plant at the 17th Avenue site. The archbishop helped St. Cecilia Parish cope with its population growth by partitioning off the eastern portion of the parish in 1929 to form St. Brendan Parish.

Even in those difficult financial times, with many parishioners out of work or concerned about the stability of their positions, Father Harnett was able to persuade them to look to the future. In 1930, the parish achieved its next goal of opening an L-shaped elementary school at the corner of 18th Avenue and Vicente Street with eight classrooms, a principal's office and a cafeteria, for the cost of $70,900. Father Harnett also raised the money to build a new rectory at 2555 17th Avenue, with enough space for a pastor, three assistants and one guest room. He was also able to obtain the services of the

Father John Harnett (1873–1946), second pastor of St. Cecilia Parish, 1929–46. *Parish Archives.*

The original school building, plus the sand lot, at corner of 17th Avenue and Vicente, mid-1940s. Note that the old 17th Avenue church building extended beyond the rectory, almost to the rear wall of the convent, which was built in 1941. *Parish Archives.*

The sixth grade of St. Cecilia School in 1930–31, posing in front of the unfinished north-facing wall of the original school building. *Parish Archives.*

Sisters of the Holy Names of Jesus and Mary to staff the school, initially housing the Sisters in the former rectory at 2562 17th Avenue.

Just as in the early days of the parish, when America's involvement in World War I did not deter the building of new parish buildings, so, too, the onset of the Great Depression did not stand in the way of expanding the parish facilities with a school and a rectory. This remains a strong example of the faith of St. Cecilia parishioners.

Looking at images of the St. Cecilia School sixth-grade class from the 1930–31 school year, we realize that most of those youngsters were born in about 1919 and were part of the earliest baby boom in the history of St. Cecilia Parish—a phenomenon that would repeat itself in coming years.

Realizing the severely cramped conditions of housing ten Sisters (one per grade level, plus a principal and a music teacher) in a modest single-family home, Father Harnett again turned to the parishioners, and by 1941, just prior to the U.S. entry into World War II, funds had been raised for construction of a three-story convent building facing 18th Avenue, with space for twenty-two Sisters—since there were already discussions underway for an expansion of the school building that would include two classes at each grade level.

Overcrowding was still an issue at Sunday Mass, as well as daily in the school building. With builders like Doelger, Costello, McKeon, Galli and others filling up block after block of sand dunes with new housing, it became clear that the land all the way to the Pacific Ocean would one day be filled with homes and businesses. At the time, the majority of new residents were Catholic families with school-age children.

With a view to this ongoing growth, Archbishop Mitty made the decision to establish the parish of St. Gabriel in 1941 by partitioning off the western portion of St. Cecilia Parish, from 28th Avenue all the way to the Pacific Ocean. Although this move helped to relieve some of the Sunday morning overcrowding at St. Cecilia Church, the parish facilities would have to be adequate "for the duration" of a great global war. However, there was still a lingering desire on the part of everyone for an expanded school and a larger, permanent church building.

PERSONAL REMINISCENCE: DONOHUE FAMILY

My siblings and I grew up on the 2600 block of 17th Avenue and attended St. Cecilia School from the 1930s until graduation in the early 1940s. The school had no kindergarten at the time, and even the word *kindergarten* had some negative overtones, since so many of our parents had been through World War I and the anti-German sentiments of that era. St. Anne of the Sunset school had a program called Pre-Primer, which was designed to get children into the classroom at an early age, prior to the introduction of the primer—the book of reading that was then used in first grade. My parents sent us there and were very happy a short time later when openings came up at St. Cecilia School—there was overcrowding even then—and we were enrolled in classrooms that held *sixty* students, with only a single nun in charge!

The 1934 First Communion group in front of the 17th Avenue church shows the tremendous increase in the population of school-age children in the parish during the 1920s and early 1930s. *Parish Archives.*

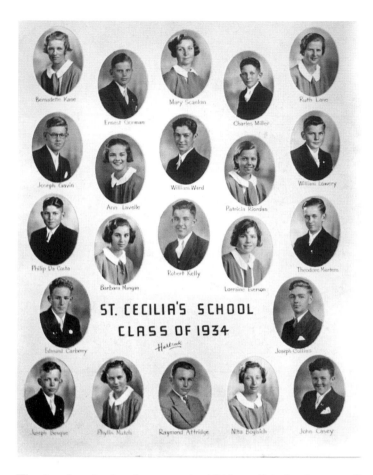

The size of graduating classes remained fairly small during the years of the Great Depression. *Parish Archives.*

PERSONAL REMINISCENCE: JOSEPHINE DUNNIGAN (1880–1960)

When I moved to St. Cecilia Parish with my two sons in 1937, the old 17th Avenue church was less than ten years old. In those early days, the seating consisted of "pop-up"–style chairs that had been donated by an old movie theater, and the kneelers were fabric squares sewn together and filled with sand—many people complained about flea bites after a Sunday morning in church! Things became a little more comfortable after Monsignor Collins completed some renovations, including adding more seating downstairs in 1949 to relieve the overcrowding at Sunday Mass. We were all very happy when our new church was dedicated in 1956.

Left: Sister Mary Anthony, a very popular sixth-grade teacher, poses with students at the end of the 1938–39 school year. In the background is the unfinished north-facing wall of the original eight-classroom school building prior to the 1948 expansion. *Parish Archives.*

Right: Sister Helen Dolores, music teacher at St. Cecilia School, photographed on Vicente Street at the end of the school year in June 1939. Sadly, Sister went to be with the Lord just four months later on October 20, 1939. The ice plant–covered sand lot in the background would become home to the new church building in a far distant future. *Parish Archives.*

THE BLESSING BEFORE MEALS
+ *Bless us, O Lord, and these Thy gifts, which we are about to receive from Thy bounty, through Christ our Lord.*
Amen.

GRACE AFTER MEALS
+ *We give Thee thanks for all Thy benefits, O Almighty God, who livest and reignest forever, and may the souls of the faithful departed through the mercy of God, rest in peace.*
Amen.

By the 1940s, most classes had increased to sixty students per grade, reflecting the growth of the neighborhood. Amazingly, there was just one Sister covering each of those eight classrooms! In spite of the "mature" look on some of these graduates, all were about fourteen years old. Today, the graduates from this photo who are still with us are approaching age ninety. *Courtesy Dolores Bosque Kelly-Hons.*

For many Catholic school graduates, the blessing before meals was one of the first religious exercises memorized during the early school years. It still rolls off the tongues of millions of Catholics of a certain age when asked to say grace before Thanksgiving dinner. The after-meal prayer was used to a lesser extent following the lunch period.

St. Cecilia School: Facts and Figures

- By the late 1920s, St. Cecilia Parish had grown from fifty-nine registered households a decade earlier to nearly six hundred—most of them with children of elementary school age, highlighting the need for a parish school.
- St. Cecilia School opened for the 1930–31 school year on August 11, 1930, with 203 students enrolled in Grades 1 through 6, with an average class size of 34 students, and fully staffed by Holy Names Sisters, including a full-time music teacher—a small nod to the background of the parish's namesake saint.

- *Some of the early enrollments in St. Cecilia School were children from Holy Name Parish (established in 1925 but without a parish school until 1941), St. Brendan Parish (established in 1929 but without a parish school until 1947) and St. Gabriel Parish (established in 1941 but without a parish school until 1948).*
- *Grade 7 was added to St. Cecilia School in the 1931–32 school year.*
- *Grade 8 was added to St. Cecilia School in the 1932–33 school year.*
- *By the late 1930s, St. Cecilia School had 480 students, with one class of 60 students at each of the eight grade levels and with one sister in charge of each class and no classroom aides.*
- *Until the 1939–40 school year, the teacher of the school's highest grade level also served as principal.*
- *From the 1940–41 school year through the 1944–45 school year, the role of principal became a separate assignment without regular classroom duties. In the 1945–46 school year, the principal once again covered a regular classroom assignment in addition to her duties as principal.*

Personal Reminiscence: Rene Herrerias

In 1945, when my brother and I were in college at USF, my parents, Juan and Amelia Herrerias, bought a home on 18th Avenue between Vicente and Wawona Streets. We had been living on California Street, where my brother and I attended St. Dominic School, and then graduated from the old St. Ignatius High School on Stanyan Street. I was fortunate enough to be part of the championship USF basketball team in 1949–50, and I still remember the shared excitement of all our friends and neighbors in St. Cecilia Parish at the time of the team's victory. My parents returned to Mexico City several years later and lived out their retirement years there, but my brother and I raised our families here in California. I'm now retired after a long teaching career and serving as head basketball coach at UC Berkeley from 1960 to 1968. I just turned ninety years old, and my wonderful wife passed away ten years ago, so I am now living at a retirement community in Walnut Creek, where I'm still able to play golf and be near my six children and many grandchildren and great-grandchildren, but I will always remember the wonderful times we had at St. Cecilia's with Monsignor Collins.

The 1944 First Communion group, photographed in the hall beneath the old 17th Avenue church. *Courtesy Grimley family.*

PERSONAL REMINISCENCE: DELPHINE STREHL JOHNSON

My sister Virginia and I grew up on 14th Avenue near Vicente and attended St. Cecilia School in the late 1930s and early 1940s. In the midst of World War II, the third-grade teacher, Sister Mary Benigna, needed a long-term substitute teacher. During this time, many things were changing, and it was a difficult time for the Sisters to staff the many areas where they were needed. She asked a longtime parishioner and friend—our mother, Claire Strehl, who had graduated from St. Rose Academy and then from UC Berkeley with a teaching credential in 1928—if she would do her the favor, and Mother agreed, becoming the first lay teacher in the history of St. Cecilia School. It was just by coincidence that my sister, Virginia, was also in that third-grade class. When it became report card time, Mother graded Virginia with mostly "B" grades, not wanting to show any partiality to her own daughter. When she showed the report cards to Sister Benigna, Sister promptly changed Virginia's grades to straight As. Mother was later hired as a permanent teacher at St. Cecilia, but after a few years, St. Gabriel School was about to open. It eventually became the largest parochial elementary school west of Chicago, with three classes of 50 students each at every grade level—a total enrollment of 1,200 children. Mother was asked to teach at the new school, and she accepted and remained there for twenty-five years until her retirement in 1972. She was among the first lay teachers in the San Francisco parochial school system, thus paving the way for many after her, and she was well known and well loved by her students and their parents.

Q. Who made the world?
A. God made the world.

Q. Who is God?
A. God is the Creator of heaven and earth, and of all things.

Q. What is man?
A. Man is a creature composed of body and soul, and made to the image and likeness of God.

Q. Why did God make you?
A. God made me to know Him, to love Him, and to serve Him in this world, and to be happy with Him forever in the next.

From the earliest days until fairly recent times, religion was always the first subject of the day, and these questions and answers from the Baltimore Catechism were always covered in the early grades.

The clapper was a small wooden device for calling students to order. It was standard issue to nuns and to some lay teachers from the 1930s until the 1970s. *Courtesy Mary Ellen (MER) Ring.*

PERSONAL REMINISCENCE: JOAN DONOHUE

The United States entered World War II just before Christmas of my eighth-grade year. Two of my classmates, Kay Allio and Dolores Bosque, joined me in producing a public-spirited community newsletter for parishioners and for those in uniform overseas. The idea came from two wonderful priests assigned to St. Cecilia at the time: Father Thomas Walsh and Father Walter Doyle. Each Sunday, parishioners were encouraged to place a handwritten note with news of their family members into the collection basket. In eighth grade and all through our high school years, the girls and I would then type these messages, run the pages off on a mimeograph machine and mail the newsletter overseas to those in the service. We began this project early in 1942 and continued through the end of the war in the summer of 1945. The newsletter was called *The Link*, and there was an image of the rosary surrounding the front page of each issue. After the war, many of those returning home thanked us for keeping them informed of life in the parish during those years.

Father Harnett served during a difficult period, arriving at St. Cecilia Parish just a few months prior to the start of the Great Depression and ending his service to the community when he went to be with the Lord less than one year after the conclusion of World War II.

Although he has been gone for decades, his legacy remains today: a physical plant to which he added a school, a convent and a rectory—all modest in size but fully paid for—along with $70,000 in the bank (a tremendous amount considering that homes in the neighborhood were selling for barely $10,000 at the time) for the use of his successor.

The 1967 Golden Jubilee book tells us, "On May 19, 1946, after a lingering illness, Father Harnett died, as quietly as he had lived, with no grand fanfare of a funeral, but with a living monument of accomplishment." More than seventy years later, we all owe him a tremendous debt of gratitude.

PERSONAL REMINISCENCE: JACQUELINE LANE (1929–2011)

My parents moved our family to a new home on 24th Avenue in the Sunset District in 1939. In those days, "parish boundaries" were fairly rigid, and you were expected to attend Mass at your assigned parish church. For whatever reason, Mother always preferred going to Sunday Mass at St. Cecilia's, especially after the arrival of Monsignor Collins in 1946. He was very kind to my parents, who were his age and who knew him from their days together at Mission Dolores. Even though we lived "outside the parish," Monsignor Collins allowed us to hold their funerals at St. Cecilia's. I continued going to Mass there after my parents were gone, eventually becoming a parishioner myself after Monsignor Harriman's arrival in 1994.

Author's note: Miss Lane's 2011 funeral was held in Our Lady's Chapel, her favorite spot for Sunday Mass.

Chapter 4

THE MONSIGNOR COLLINS ERA

1946–1976

I t began quietly enough with a brief announcement at Sunday Mass on December 29, 1946. Parishioners were invited to a small afternoon reception to meet the new pastor. Little could those attendees have imagined the changes that lay ahead for themselves and for the parish of St. Cecilia on that long-ago post-Christmas Sunday afternoon. Monsignor Collins's appointment as pastor was only one of many changes that began to emerge in the post–World War II years.

PERSONAL REMINISCENCE: JOHN F. DUNNIGAN (1913–1988)

When our family moved to St. Cecilia Parish in 1937, we lived on 21st Avenue near Rivera. The country was just coming out of the Great Depression, and money was still tight for many people. It was the custom of many churches in those days for a plate of coins to be passed around the congregation just prior to the Sunday collection, so that those attending Mass might make change for dollar bills, since very few people were well off enough at that time to contribute a full dollar every Sunday. This system worked well for years, but once Monsignor Collins arrived at the end of 1946, inflation was beginning to raise the prices of everything—utilities, janitorial, groceries for the rectory and the convent, etc. Monsignor immediately eliminated the "change plate" and declared that he was looking for a "silent collection" every

Sunday—that is, paper money only and no coins. He explained the reasons for this, and most people understood and went along with his suggestion, thus bolstering parish finances at a critical time.

Author's note: Some pastors in the San Francisco archdiocese have been forced to issue the same reminder nearly seventy years later!

Just as in the post–World War I era, the parish was growing, as veterans returned home, married and started families. Sunday Mass attendance continued to increase, and with the relaxation of gasoline rationing in 1946, Americans began driving more than ever before. Nowhere was this particular change more apparent than at Sunday Mass, where parking problems were painfully evident. Monsignor Collins decided early in his tenure that the sand lot at the northwest corner of 17th Avenue and Vicente Street would be paved to provide additional parking for Sunday Mass attendees and ease the situation for the church's neighbors.

The overcrowding inside the 17th Avenue church was also a problem. This led to the creation of a "lower church" by converting the parish hall in the church basement into a fully functioning "lower church," thus adding enough seating to accommodate another 544 worshippers, bringing the church's combined capacity to approximately 1,000 seats. New foam-rubber kneelers were also added, eliminating the problem of fleas in the old sand-filled kneelers.

PERSONAL REMINISCENCE: DOLORES BOSQUE KELLY-HONS
After World War II, Monsignor Collins arrived in the parish, and he was a very big supporter of the Tobin Club—a social group for young adults, many of whom were returning home once the war ended. The boys were very happy to have a place to socialize, and the girls seemed to like it a lot, as well. Monsignor only half-jokingly called it his "Marriage Bureau" and was always very pleased when members became engaged to one another. The club was so successful that within a few years it was disbanded, since almost all of the active members were married by then. Monsignor knew that babies would soon follow, and in 1948,

> he doubled the size of the school to make room for the children who were part of the postwar baby boom—many of whose parents met one another through his Tobin Club.

As part of the renovation of the 17th Avenue church building, Monsignor Collins was pleased to accept a gift of a new tabernacle from parishioners Mr. and Mrs. Chris McKeon, given in honor of their son and other young men from the parish who died in World War II. That memorial tabernacle was moved to the new church, where it still houses the Blessed Sacrament today.

Right: The Tobin Club was a parish social group that provided activities for young adults after World War II. *Courtesy Dolores Bosque Kelly-Hons.*

Below: Tobin Club dinner gathering, 1949. Chaplain Father Eugene Gallagher is seated at center. In spite of the "mature" look of many members, virtually all were in their twenties at the time. *Courtesy Dolores Bosque Kelly-Hons.*

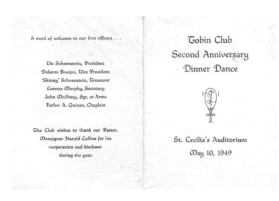

A word of welcome to our first officers . . .

Vic Schoenstein, President
Dolores Bosque, Vice President
'Skinny' Schoenstein, Treasurer
Loretta Murphy, Secretary
John McGinty, Sgt. at Arms
Father A. Quinan, Chaplain

The Club wishes to thank our Pastor, Monsignor Harold Collins for his cooperation and kindness during the year.

Tobin Club
Second Anniversary
Dinner Dance

St. Cecilia's Auditorium
May 10, 1949

PERSONAL REMINISCENCE: MONSIGNOR HAROLD E. COLLINS
March 30, 1947

The new tabernacle, donated by Mr. and Mrs. Chris McKeon, was solemnly blessed and dedicated to the loving memory of the following boys who died in the service during World War II:

Jerome Argenti	Chris McKeon Jr.
Raymond M. Beach	Adolph A. Meier
Philip Crimmins	George F. Read
George Ehrmann	Ralph Schoenstein
Warren Goepp	Edmund Scully
Robert Halleran	John Sullivan
Charles V. Haven	Robert Von der Mehden

Taken from Monsignor Collins's handwritten notes of Sunday announcements, bound in thirty volumes (1946–76) and part of St. Cecilia Parish Archives.

Watching the Sunday afternoon church schedule, which often included half a dozen or more baptisms between 2:00 p.m. and 4:00 p.m. on Sunday afternoons, Monsignor Collins quickly identified another huge change in the making: the postwar baby boom was well underway in St. Cecilia Parish.

Plans were made and funds raised, and the 18th Avenue expansion of the school building—doubling the school's capacity and costing $300,000—was soon completed and dedicated on February 1, 1948—little more than one year after the appointment of Monsignor Collins as pastor. With the convent capable of holding twenty-two nuns, additional Sisters were assigned to St. Cecilia School, and several laywomen were also recruited as permanent additions to the teaching staff.

Monsignor Collins was keenly aware of the devoted service of the Sisters of the Holy Names of Jesus and Mary. Plans for the school expansion also included a walled garden around the convent for the Sisters' recreation. There was also a covered walkway built from the northwest corner entrance of the school, along 18th Avenue, and then entering the convent's walled garden. Today, we must remember the importance of these small amenities—for the Sisters needed to return to the privacy of the convent periodically during their workday, for meals and to "excuse themselves." Many students recall that in those days, the Sisters were never seen even using a school drinking fountain!

ST. CECILIA SCHOOL: FACTS AND FIGURES

- *From the 1945–46 school year through the 1949–50 school year, the principal once again covered a regular classroom assignment in addition to her duties as principal.*
- *The first lay teacher, Mrs. Claire Strehl, was hired in 1943 as a substitute teacher during World War II. She was then hired as the first permanent lay teacher in 1946, in anticipation of the school's upcoming expansion in the 1947–48 school year.*
- *The expanded school building was formally dedicated on February 1, 1948.*
- *Kindergarten was introduced in the 1948–49 school year, after the school building's expansion.*
- *Beginning in the 1950–51 school year, the role of principal was permanently established to include no regular classroom assignment.*
- *By the late 1940s, costs had begun to rise, and the decision was made to allow for monthly payments once the school's annual tuition exceeded twenty-five dollars per year per student.*
- *By the mid-1950s, tuition was set at five dollars per month per family (regardless of how many children) for the ten months of the school year. For many years, some families—Bosque, Moriarty, O'Callaghan, Igoa, Buick, Pengel, Harrington, Uribe, McKeon and others—had five or more children enrolled in the parish school at the same time.*
- *The school's peak enrollment was reached in the 1952–53 school year, with 886 students taught by sixteen Sisters and one lay teacher, with an average class size of 52.*
- *Due to the ever-increasing number of students in K–8 classes (sometimes a few more than the standard fifty of that era), the school began to exceed its fire department–rated capacity of eight hundred students, and the decision was reluctantly made to close the kindergarten beginning in the fall of 1957. This action was taken in order to comply with new archdiocesan regulations limiting class size and also fire safety guidelines.*
- *In the 1950s and 1960s, about 10 percent of the mothers of students at St. Cecilia School worked outside the home. By 1973, this figure had jumped to 40 percent, and within a decade, it was 70 percent. By 2015, it was estimated that 95 percent of the mothers were working for pay outside the home.*

- *In the summer of 1960, Monsignor Collins had the entire school building (hallways, classrooms, cafeteria and auditorium) retrofitted with automatic fire sprinklers in response to a tragic December 1958 fire at a Catholic elementary school in Chicago that claimed the lives of ninety-two students and three nuns.*
- *By the early 1960s, tuition at St. Cecilia School had increased to six dollars per month per family for the ten months of the school year.*
- *By the late 1960s, tuition had increased to eight dollars per month per family for the ten months of the school year.*
- *For many years, there was an effort made to cap the number of lay teachers at four (five with kindergarten included), although by the late 1960s, the number of lay teachers was growing.*
- *The first male lay teacher, Mr. Thomas Kennedy, was hired in the 1967–68 school year.*
- *In that same 1967–68 school year, several of the Sisters began to use their baptismal and family names for the first time instead of the names taken at the time of their religious vows.*
- *Also in the 1967–68 school year, several of the Sisters began wearing a modified habit consisting of a knee-length skirt, white blouse, vest and short veil.*
- *In the 1968–69 school year, the first principal was appointed who chose to use her birth and family names.*
- *In the 1969–70 school year, the faculty was evenly divided between Holy Names Sisters and lay teachers, both female and male.*
- *By the 1971–72 school year, lay teachers, both female and male, had begun to outnumber the Sisters.*
- *By the 1972–73 school year, there were only five Sisters remaining who were assigned full-time classroom duties.*
- *In the 1973–74 school year, there were 613 children enrolled in sixteen classrooms, with an average class size of 38.*

Another innovation implemented by Monsignor Collins in the late 1940s was the Parish Festival, held each fall in the new auditorium of the expanded school building. Over the years, themes varied considerably from one year to the next: European Holiday, Wild West, Hawaiian Adventures and dozens of others. In the early years of the festival, with the deprivations caused by World War II rationing clearly in the minds of many parishioners, prizes

A long line of nuns and priests walk from the 17th Avenue church through an honor guard of students to the schoolyard, where Monsignor Collins and hundreds of guests were waiting for dedication ceremonies to begin for the expanded school building on February 1, 1948. Note the paved parking lot—a new innovation that replaced a sand dune just one year earlier. *Parish Archives.*

Well-dressed evening crowd at the 1948 Parish Festival in the newly constructed school auditorium. *Parish Archives.*

A 1948 festival hat booth staffed by parishioners. *Parish Archives.*

were often as simple as a pound of bacon, a two-pound can of coffee or a five-pound sack of sugar. Parishioners came together to have fun, socialize and, most importantly, support the parish school. Today, the annual festival remains one of the school's most consistent fundraisers, thereby keeping tuition costs within the means of many families.

PERSONAL REMINISCENCE: DORIS GRIMLEY

My father's parents were early residents of St. Cecilia Parish, living on Claremont near the West Portal entrance to the Twin Peaks Tunnel. I grew up on 21st Avenue near Vicente and graduated from St. Cecilia School in 1950. Once Monsignor Collins became pastor just after World War II, he took on the task of distributing report cards while seated at the front of the classroom. He and my father had been classmates at Mission Dolores School right after the earthquake and fire of 1906, and he always said that my father was the smartest boy in their class.

He embarrassed me at report card time by asking me, "Who was the smartest boy in my class at Mission Dolores?" and I had to say, "It was my father, Monsignor." Other children were on the spot to explain a low grade in Religion or Courtesy, but he reminded me every time what a smart father I had. He was a wonderful man with great people skills, and he remembered small details like this about every family in the parish.

By the mid-1950s, however, with the postwar baby boom in full swing, the situation had become critical. Even though the school had sixty children per classroom prior to 1948, the postwar goal in the expanded building was forty-five per classroom, with eighty children enrolled in kindergarten (forty in the morning session and another forty in the afternoon session). With this arrangement in place, the school was in compliance with its San Francisco Fire Department–rated capacity of eight hundred students. Difficulties

The old 17th Avenue Church was located just north of the rectory, where the parking lot stands today. Image from Christmas 1950. *Parish Archives.*

Investiture of new altar servers at Sunday Mass in the old 17th Avenue church, about 1950. *Parish Archives.*

Once the expanded school building was completed in 1948, the student population soon exceeded eight hundred students. Note the lighted Christmas trees in each classroom and the street-level Nativity scene from Christmas 1950. *Parish Archives.*

Above: School uniforms, shown here in the early 1950s, have changed several times over the years. Not all of these students seem happy with the new style. *Parish Archives.*

Right: The 1952 baptism of Christine Marie Ruck in the old 17th Avenue Church, with Father Felix Flynn officiating. The "baby," who is now of retirement age, remains a St. Cecilia parishioner today. *Ruck family photo.*

began to emerge, as the higher grades were gradually acquiring a few extra students each year—the school always attempted to accommodate all siblings in a family. In addition, the tuition structure of the time—five dollars per month per family—encouraged siblings to attend the same school. The issue came to a head just before the 1957 school year when it was finally realized that with fifty students in each of the sixteen classrooms for Grades 1 through 8, and another eighty-plus students divided between morning and afternoon kindergarten, the school was seriously exceeding its legal capacity. Knowing that it was impossible to reduce the sizes of any of the existing classes, Monsignor Collins reluctantly agreed to close the kindergarten class at the end of the 1956–57 school year. Due to ongoing fire regulations, as well as later archdiocese-mandated reductions in class size, it would be nearly twenty-five years before kindergarten could be reopened.

PERSONAL REMINISCENCE: MARY SCANLON, PARISH SECRETARY
In the 1950s and 1960s, the parish often had two or three weddings scheduled every Saturday, especially during the busy summer months, along with five or more baptisms on Sunday afternoons throughout the entire year. With nine Masses every Sunday morning and nearly five thousand people in attendance, plus confessions on Saturday afternoons and before every single Sunday Mass, along with all those weddings and baptisms, plus sick calls at all hours, the priests were exhausted by dinnertime on Sunday night.

Monsignor Collins was proud of the changes that he was able to implement in his first year as pastor, but the biggest was yet to come. Ever since the parish's founding in 1917, there had been hopes for a "permanent" church building. Each of the early churches had been regarded as "temporary" until funds were available to build something larger and more substantial. Finally, the time had come, and on New Year's Day 1952, Archbishop Mitty formally consented to the parish's request to build a new St. Cecilia Church.

Monsignor Collins quickly organized door-to-door teams to solicit financial pledges from parishioners, and on May 30, 1954, he donned a hard hat and climbed into the cab of a steam shovel to break ground for the new church.

Monsignor Collins was a highly successful fundraiser for St. Cecilia Parish. Here he is reviewing the organizational structure of the building fund campaign with volunteer Martin Ruane in 1952. It would be two more years before the groundbreaking ceremonies. *Parish Archives.*

Beanie and block worn by school cheerleaders at the St. Cecilia–Holy Name sports tournament, February 28, 1954. *Courtesy Carolyn Meagher Hewes.*

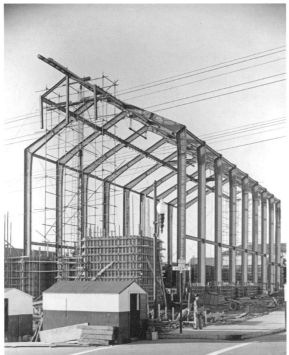

Above: The beginning of the fulfillment of a dream—construction begins on the first "permanent" church for St. Cecilia Parish. The paved parking lot installed in 1947 had already been excavated (see debris piled adjacent to school building), and members of the St. Cecilia Band and Drum Corps were out in force. Monsignor Collins, standing just right of center, was about to enter the cab of a steam shovel to break ground for construction activities on May 30, 1954. *Parish Archives.*

Left: The steel frame rises in late 1954. Construction workers installed a Christmas tree, visible for miles, from the top girder. *San Francisco History Center, San Francisco Public Library.*

St. Cecilia Parish in the News
On December 16, 1954, **San Francisco Chronicle** *columnist Dick Friendlich wrote the following: "Eye-catcher at 17ᵗʰ Avenue and Vicente where the steel girders for the new St. Cecilia's Church rise some 70 feet into the air. Jacks and Irvine, the construction outfit, have put a Christmas tree on the top girders and strung it with lights. Visible for miles..."*

In that post–World War II era, urban planners envisioned a freeway link from San Francisco International Airport to the Golden Gate Bridge in what essentially was a straight line. Such a project would have destroyed the unity of St. Cecilia Parish with a wall of concrete. The freeway would have destroyed hundreds of homes and businesses in its path, as it moved through the West Portal shopping area before following a path between 14ᵗʰ and 15ᵗʰ Avenues. The new St. Cecilia Church, which was then under construction at 17ᵗʰ Avenue and Vicente just two blocks away, would have suffered from the noise and debris while becoming isolated from those parishioners living east of 15ᵗʰ Avenue. Monsignor Collins declared "war" on the State of California and rallied his troops from all walks of life to attend a massive public hearing at Lincoln High School on a cold December night in 1955 to denounce the plan. After much deliberation, the politicians agreed with the people, and the freeway plan was eventually scrapped once and for all.

In the course of planning the new St. Cecilia Church, Monsignor Collins was especially concerned with the interior elements such as pews, confessionals, the Communion rail, statues, the crucifix over the main altar and so on. In his scholarly textbook on church construction, *The Church: Its Edifice and Appointments*, a standard reference work for more than thirty years, Monsignor Collins cited the words of another author on the subject of Catholic church décor: "With remarkable frequency one may find plaster-casts from the same foreign molds. Statues of this well-known type have no architectural qualities; only by courtesy can they be described as works of ecclesiastical art." With this thought in mind, Monsignor Collins determined that there would be something better for the new St. Cecilia Church.

He engaged the services of Sunset District resident Samuel Berger as the official wood carver for the church proect. Mr. Berger, who had been born in Bucharest in 1886, was trained in the royal palace of the

Right: The State of California's 1955 freeway plan would have built a concrete wall through the middle of the parish. Monsignor Collins vowed that this would never happen. *Courtesy Eric Fischer.*

Below: Construction progress, as workers lay radiant heating lines on the floor of the new church building, 1955. *Parish Archives.*

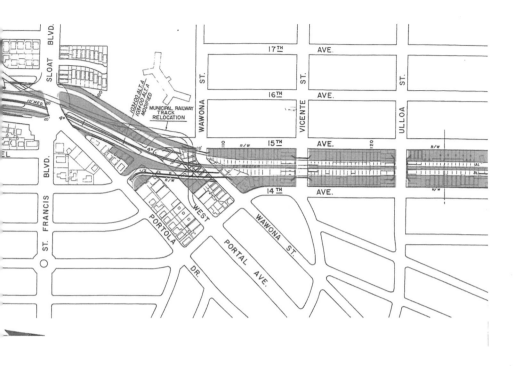

king of Romania. Fleeing Jewish persecution, Mr. Berger arrived in San Francisco as a young man in 1904. Finding ample work in his profession after the 1906 earthquake/fire, Mr. Berger and his skilled workers, operating from a downtown studio, were much in demand for rebuilding houses of worship that had been lost, as well as the construction of new churches in the city's western neighborhoods.

Mr. Berger's style involved developing sketches with the client before undertaking any carving. Some of his firm's work was completed in San Francisco, and some was contracted out. Clients often chose to have statues and icons painted, and these frequently resembled stone carvings. Mr. Berger's work is featured in many local institutions, including Mission Dolores Basilica, the Carmelite Convent of Cristo Rey, St. Ignatius Church, St. Anne, St. Brigid, Star of the Sea Churches, Grace Cathedral, Temple Emanu-El, St. Catherine of Siena Church in Burlingame and Santa Clara University.

As the foundation was poured that summer, the steel frame soon rose high above the neighboring homes. Construction progressed at a steady pace throughout 1955, and on Pentecost Sunday, May 20, 1956, the new St. Cecilia Church was dedicated in an elaborate ceremony led by

This wood carving of the Blessed Mother statue, prepared by Samuel Berger, was eventually placed at the front of the new church, on the left side, where it remains to this day. *Courtesy Lynn Goldfinger-Abram.*

Monsignor Collins and San Francisco Archbishop John J. Mitty, along with thousands of happy parishioners. Less than two years after the groundbreaking ceremony, the Parkside District had a new landmark, visible for miles across the city.

Right: One of the first weddings in the "new church" was that of twenty-one-year-old St. Cecilia School alum Beverly Meagher and her fiancé, Bernie Paulsen, on September 1, 1956. Note the well-hatted female guests in the congregation. *Paulsen family photo.*

Below: A youthful Father James P. McKay in the schoolyard, late 1950s, during his initial assignment to St. Cecilia Church as a parish priest and assistant pastor (1956–62). *Lynch family photo.*

The coming of Hawaiian statehood prompted the theme of the 1959 Parish Festival. *Parish Archives.*

PERSONAL REMINISCENCE: CHRISTINE MEAGHER KELLER

I remember being very excited to be a four-year-old flower girl when my older sister Beverly was married at the new St. Cecilia Church in September of 1956. I was still two years away from attending first grade, and like many of the children in our generation, I had siblings who were much older—there was a seventeen-year age difference between my oldest sister and myself. All of us attended school at St. Cecilia, and my next sister, Carolyn, was married at St. Cecilia Church in 1969. In 1974, my father walked me down that same aisle, eighteen years after Bev's wedding—by then, he had accumulated plenty of practice!

The Monsignor Collins Era

Remembering the 1957 Earthquake

Compiled by Jo Anne Quinn

There was an entire series of small earthquakes that Friday morning—the first at 10:26 a.m., another about twenty minutes later, another just after that and then another one just before eleven o'clock, another just after eleven and a sixth one at 11:19 a.m. Less than half an hour later came the biggest one that San Francisco had experienced in half a century.

The clock on the Ferry Building stopped running for the first time since April 18, 1906. It was fifteen minutes before noon, Friday, March 22, 1957.

The nearby apartments at Stonestown had hundreds of broken windows, and many of the large plate glass windows in the stores also shattered. Neighborhood grocery stores saw the contents of their shelves crash to the ground, and brick chimneys and fireplaces in nearby Westlake, sitting directly on top of the San Andreas Fault, were knocked loose.

At St. Cecilia School, hundreds of students from the upper grades were packed into the lower church just before lunch on the third Friday in Lent for Stations of the Cross. Years later, in 2006, members of the class of 1960, fifth graders at the time, shared their memories.

Tom O'T: The first shake happened just after morning recess as we were going back to our classroom. The second and major shake happened just after Stations of the Cross as Father Riordan was going through the Benediction portion. After that tremendous jolt, it was evident many of us were scared and unsure what to do. Father Riordan paused, turned around, addressed us all saying something to the effect, "We just had an earthquake; it's all over; there is nothing to be afraid of. We'll continue with Benediction." Father turned back and finished in record time. He went from a '45 to a '78 recording and was off that altar in a flash. Must thank the nuns who took control and kept us relatively calm and in order.

Bob O'D: Those wildly wobbling candlesticks on the altar during the earthquake—none fell, but Tom was right: Father Riordan finished Benediction at warp speed.

Jim H: I remember being in church and watching the light fixture above me swinging. I was next to the center aisle. Instead of simply diving under the pews as some did, I was going to run if the light fixture started to fall. Cracks in the halls of the school and a pretty good aftershock while walking up the stairs to the second floor, making me use the hand rail. I don't remember any

The lower church in its original configuration, mid-1950s. Both the upper and lower church spaces were regularly filled to near capacity at the 9:00 a.m., 10:00 a.m. and 12:15 p.m. Sunday Masses from 1956 until the 1970s. At Christmas and Easter, there were literal overflows of worshippers out the doors of both church spaces. Shifting patterns of Mass attendance led Monsignor McKay to remove the pews and repurpose the space into the original Collins Center in the late 1970s. *Parish Archives.*

big statues falling. Rather, one had rotated ninety degrees—it was not facing forward anymore.

ROSALIE S: Father Riordan had beads of perspiration on his forehead that day!

KATHY K: I remember getting under the pews when the giant pillars started swaying back and forth. Also recall the tremors that followed the big one for the rest of the day. What a mess our garage was when I got home!

JOHN L: My recollection of that day is as vivid as the day it shook. We were in the lower church after Stations of the Cross, and it started shaking. Father Riordan turned to us, lifted his hands and told us to be calm, and right at that moment it stopped. We all filed out and lined up in the schoolyard. After a while, they let us go back to our classrooms, where we found all the desks in disarray and papers all over the floor. What I thought was outrageous was that some of the big statues of Mary, on pedestals in every room above the teacher's desk, fell and shattered.

JOHN M: I remember being in the lower church and all of us ducking under the pews. Then Father Riordan tried to calm us. I think I went back under the pew. I believe we had some projects in the classroom that were thrown to the floor due to the earthquake.

RITA M: My memory is very much the same, with Father Riordan finishing the Stations of the Cross at record speed and beads of sweat running down his face. However, I remember wondering why a man of the cloth was so worried and scared. Yes, we were all pretty scared, but he wasn't supposed to be! He was gone immediately, and we were left to the nuns. I remember a crack in the wall of the school, some statues broken and going home scared, to find things in disarray.

JO ANNE Q: Ah! The earthquake! We were all herded into the yard. Parents were called to come take us home. One kid got hysterical—knelt down, put an ear to the ground and started screaming that he could hear "the earth cracking and popping." That started a lot of other kids screaming, and the nuns had to quell the impending riot. When I got home, there were more tremors, and a tall, heavy bookcase nearly came down on my mother! I must have been ahead of my time, because I indulged in "play therapy." Got out my dollhouse, set it up with furniture and its little people and then shook the heck out of it!

JERRY F: I think it was Steve D. who put his ear to the ground to listen for another earthquake. I remember thinking it was really a goofy thing to do, and it somehow scared me, but in retrospect it was probably about the most scientific thing a fifth grader could do to predict another quake. This was not much removed from what's happening now, with probes in the ground for earthquake detection, right?

EDNA L: I was still at Parkside School awaiting a spot at St. Cecilia's. I remember sitting on a chair at my desk in the middle section of the classroom. And after it stopped shaking, I was still on the chair but now over against the wall. They sent everyone home and didn't bother to call parents. There were kids whose parents worked, and they had to go home alone. I lived across the

Sister Eileen Catharine (later known as Sister Kathleen McDonough) and students John Mullane and Charles Shea at Larsen Park, 19th Avenue and Ulloa Street, at the end of the school year in 1957. Sister lived to be eighty-five years old, returning to the Lord in March 2016. *San Francisco History Center, San Francisco Public Library.*

EUCHARISTIC FAST REGULATIONS FOR THE LAITY

1) Water never breaks the fast.
2) It is necessary to fast from solid foods and from alcoholic beverages for three hours before receiving Holy Communion; non-alcoholic beverages may be taken up to one hour before Communion.
3) These regulations must be followed at any time that Holy Communion is received, i.e., whether it be at morning Mass, Evening Mass, or Midnight Mass.
4) The sick, even those who are not bedridden, are permitted to take true and proper medicine (either liquid or solid) and non-alcoholic beverages at any time before receiving Holy Communion.
5) The laity no longer have to consult a priest before availing themselves of these concessions.

FAST AND ABSTINENCE REGULATIONS

CHART OF DAYS OF FAST AND ABSTINENCE — PERSONS	(1) FAST ONLY	(2) FAST AND PARTIAL ABSTINENCE	(3) FAST AND ABSTINENCE	(4) ABSTINENCE ONLY
	All Weekdays of Lent, except: Ash Wednesday, Fridays, and Ember Wednesday and Saturday.	Ember Wednesday & Saturday; Vigil of Pentecost.	Fridays of Lent; Ember Fridays; Ash Wednesday; Dec. 7; Dec. 24.	All Fridays of Year, except: Fridays of Lent, and Ember Friday.
Under 7	No Fast No Abstinence	No Fast No Abstinence	No Fast No Abstinence	No Fast No Abstinence
Over 7 and Under 21; or Over 59	No Fast No Abstinence (4)	No Fast Meat Once	No Fast No Meat	No Fast No Meat
Over 21 and Under 59	Fast Meat Once	Fast Meat Once	Fast No Meat	No Fast No Meat

1) On days of FAST, only one full meal allowed. Two other meatless meals may be taken according to one's needs; but together they should not equal another full meal.
2) On days of Partial Abstinence, meat and soup or gravy made from meat may be taken ONCE A DAY at the PRINCIPAL MEAL, even by those not obliged to fast.
3) On days of COMPLETE ABSTINENCE, no meat or meat-soup or gravy may be taken.
4) Persons not obliged to FAST may eat meat several times on DAYS OF FAST which are not also DAYS OF ABSTINENCE.
NB: All over 7 are bound to abstinence; all over 21 and under 59 are bound to FAST, unless exempt or dispensed. In case of doubt, consult your Parish Priest or Confessor.

Regulations regarding fasting and abstinence were far more restrictive in 1958 than today. Such rules presented many challenges to those responsible for preparing family meals, as the restrictions were vastly different, depending on the ages, occupations and health of various family members. *Parish Archives.*

street from Parkside, so I brought some kids home with me until they could get ahold of their parents. I remember all of the stonework on every house on the block was broken away, having fallen to the ground.

Maureen M: Walking home after that earthquake and seeing the 16th Avenue and Taraval Market with all the windows broken.

Diane F: They let us go home early, and I was so nervous that I ate meat on Friday! My mom said it was okay—God wouldn't punish us again!

And the best recollection of all:

Pam B: I remember my mother picking me up at school after the quake, taking me to the Emporium in Stonestown and buying me Elvis's record "All Shook Up."

The most frequently played recessional hymn at St. Cecilia Church from the 1950s until the 1970s was "Immaculate Mary," also known as "The Lourdes Hymn." Although the words vary somewhat in French-speaking Quebec, plus in some Spanish-speaking countries, these are the lyrics most frequently used in the United States, and often just the first verse is sung. Many parishioners can

---

St. Cecilia Parish in the News

In the fall of 1958, California voters were asked to consider Proposition 16, which would have imposed taxation on all private schools throughout the state. In a highly ecumenical gesture, Monsignor Collins rallied the voters, both within and beyond the Catholic Church, to defeat the measure. In a series of mailings, he carefully pointed out that there were more than one thousand private schools operating statewide at that time, educating more than 340,000 students. Politicians estimated a $1.8 million increase in state revenues if private schools were taxed. Monsignor Collins replied that if private schools were forced to close because of the burden of such taxation, the State of California would then be responsible for providing educations to those 340,000 students, at a cost of $350 million immediately for construction of additional school facilities, plus another $118 million in annual operating costs. The tax measure was then defeated with a resounding 70 percent "No" vote, thus reaffirming the tax-exempt status of all private schools in California.

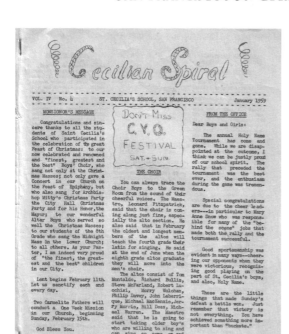

Left: The *Cecilian Spiral* was the school's news magazine in the late 1950s and early 1960s, featuring news articles and updates of what was taking place in each of the sixteen classrooms. *Author's collection.*

Below: By May 1960, the First Communion group, pictured in the school auditorium, numbered well over one hundred, fueled by the post–World War II baby boom. Monsignor Collins is seen standing at left. *Author's collection.*

still hear the organ holding forth, as Monsignor Collins led the congregation with maestro-like gestures from the pulpit at the conclusion of Sunday Mass on all those foggy Sunday mornings in a long-gone time. This song was also used as the closing hymn at the dedication of the Durocher Pavilion in May 2000.

Three friends from the 1960 First Communion class pose in front of an 18th Avenue home. *Courtesy of a private collector.*

The cover of the program for a school-wide performance in the auditorium, open to family and friends. Students at St. Cecilia School have long been accustomed to appearing onstage in musical, singing and dramatic performances. *Courtesy Jo Anne Quinn.*

"IMMACULATE MARY" ("THE LOURDES HYMN")

Immaculate, Mary!
Our hearts are on fire.
That title so wondrous
Fills all our desire!

Chorus

We pray for our Mother,
The Church upon earth.
And bless, sweetest Lady,
The land of our birth.

Chorus

For poor, sick, afflicted,
Thy mercy we crave.
And comfort the dying,
Thou, Light of the Grave.

Chorus

Immaculate, Mary!
Your praises we sing,
To God Our Father,
And Christ our King.

Chorus

Ave, Ave, Ave, Maria!
Ave, Ave, Ave, Maria!

Text: Anonymous, Parochial Hymn Book, Boston, 1897; revision of a prior work by Jeremiah Cummings (1814–1866). Music: Traditional Pyrenean melody, 1882, Grenoble, by Augustus Edmonds Tozer (1857–1910).

THE MONSIGNOR COLLINS ERA

The first teen club of St. Cecilia Parish was founded in the 1940s. It provided recent grads of the parish school with a place to socialize during the days of World War II, when many commodities—including sugar, meat, coffee, gasoline and tires—were severely rationed for the war effort. Many of the members from that era have fond recollections of teen club events as a no-cost way of socializing.

By the 1950s and 1960s, most parishes in the Archdiocese of San Francisco had active teen clubs in place—a reflection of the high birthrate in the city during the years following World War II. The Cecilian Club of St. Cecilia Parish and the Brendan Club of nearby St. Brendan Parish were among the most popular of the era, based on the success of various dances and ski trips. St. Edward's, a now-closed parish on California Street near Laurel Village, had the distinction of having a teen club, although that parish did not have an elementary school. In the words of many young people of that era, several of their friends favored membership in St. Edward's Club: "You could meet new people there who were not your classmates from all the way back in kindergarten days."

Several St. Cecilia grads and others from the 1960s were kind enough to share some of their own memorable teen club moments more than fifty years later:

> *JOANNE: My teen club memory is of the dances down in the auditorium, where the girls all stood together on one side and the boys all stood together on the other side of the room. Father Walsh would walk around encouraging us to "circulate." I only remember one ski trip when we were freshmen—I think it was to Squaw Valley. I don't remember anything horrible happening—I even recall having a pretty good time.*

> *DEBBIE: My older siblings always enjoyed teen club, so my parents urged me to go. By the 1960s, however, with the coming of rock concerts, no one wanted to folk dance in the school auditorium any more, and many of us maintained membership only so that we could go on those ski trips.*

> *FRANK: In the late 1960s, the monthly meetings were held on Tuesday nights, and everyone who had just graduated from St. Cecilia's eighth grade was automatically made a member. There was a rule that you had to telephone the rectory by 4:00 p.m. on the day of the meeting if you were*

not going to attend that month. Some of us did this faithfully, thinking that someone, somewhere, was going to put a big red check mark next to our names if we no-showed without calling first.

RAMONA: I remember being in a teen club–related play Bells Are Ringing, *which was some kind of citywide competition with other parishes. I think we won. Father Walsh took the cast out to dinner, and afterwards, some of us went to a bar on California Street or someplace…my first time in a bar and I'm a junior or senior in high school! So, not knowing what to order, I recalled the Kingston Trio's song "Scotch and Soda," so that's what I asked for—though I never drank it. Weeks later, I'm doing dishes, and my mother says, "I talked to so and so (some friend of hers), and he says he saw you in a bar…" I reply, "Me?? In a bar??? He must be mistaken…" Can't remember how many Our Fathers and Hail Marys I did for that one! I also remember getting jilted by this guy I was dating when he never showed up for one of the dances…very sad, but somehow karma payback for my misbehavior!*

MARK: Teen club ski trips…I remember bits and pieces of going to Squaw Valley via bus. Mr. O'Toole and Mr. Diner were telling me skiing was easy or some such thing and if I could snow plow I'd be able to go anywhere. They said that I didn't really need a lesson—just hop on the chair and follow them. It was an agonizing trip to the bottom of the ski area. Stopping at the Nut Tree south of Davis to get something to eat on the way home was the best part of that day.

NANCY: Seeing those Driver's Education car crash movies—"Blood on the Highway" or something like that—as Father Walsh was walking around with a pack of cigarettes in the front pocket of his short-sleeve black shirt with the Roman collar; that was a sporty look back then. There was always some girl throwing up in the bathroom or crying because some guy wouldn't talk to her or dance with her. Those dances could be fun, but it took forever for the first couple to get out on the floor to get things started.

JEAN: I went once to St Cecilia's teen club, but my memory is a bit hazy. I do remember going to St. Vincent de Paul's teen club multiple times and dancing with a lot of guys from the Marina District. I think I was misdirected, as I am sure the St. Cecilia's guys would have been better dancers with all of Mrs. Hunter's lessons.

LINDA: Girls seemed to like the monthly teen club meetings and dances more than boys. I remember that a cute junior from SI asked me to dance at a teen club event back in 1963 when I was a pretty shy Catholic high school sophomore, but it seemed to work out well for us. He and I will be celebrating our fiftieth wedding anniversary in June 2017, along with our children and grandchildren.

JO ANNE: I have few recollections of teen club…I think my parents discouraged me from going because they didn't want me hanging out too much with boys! I do remember a ski trip to Squaw Valley. The boots I rented were a little too big for me, and I had to wear lots of socks. Didn't have a clue about skiing…tried it and felt like a total dork. Halfway through the stay, I accidentally stepped on what I thought was solid ice… it was not, but rather the edge of a pond. One foot went through, and water filled my boot! I staggered around for the rest of the day in a freezing, soggy boot because I had nothing I could change into. I was miserable and very glad to get home!

BOB: I do have one large event related to the teen club. I joined the Cecilians as soon as I exited the seminary in mid-sophomore year of high school. One of the first events I attended was a ski trip to Squaw Valley. After a year and a half in the seminary, I felt I needed to catch up with my previously nonexistent social life. I somehow hooked up with an old SC classmate and while everyone else was attending a 4:00 a.m. Mass before the trip, my buddy and I decided to consume some hidden beers. Our first problem was that there was no restroom on this bus. Needless to say, by Sacramento (our first and only stop) I was in serious distress. Once we arrived and began skiing, my friend and I met some guys from another group who were drinking, and we joined them. My next recollection was waking up in the Emergency Room at Truckee Hospital. Apparently, I had fallen off a cliff into a creek bed. My friend was taller and therefore a bit more sober than I, so I guess he was the one who went for help. I was given the Last Rites (what we called Extreme Unction back then), and the priest who was in charge of the group then announced that the rest of the trip was canceled and we were headed back home immediately because of misbehavior on the part of my friend and myself. I knew that all of our friends on the bus would be very angry at both of us on the ride home, but then the priest announced that my friend and I, calling our names out loud, would not be riding back on the bus with the rest of the group—wow, what good luck! The downside was that he then told everyone that our fathers were each driving to Tahoe to pick us up—very bad things were in store for my friend and myself! I don't think Dad and I said more than three words all the way home. To make matters even worse, our car broke down in Vallejo. We then had to take a bus back into the city, arriving with the early morning commute rush. I know that the priest talked to my father before we left, and Dad continued to say nothing once we arrived at home, but later that day, both my parents together sat me down (a sure sign of big trouble) and I was grounded for a very long time afterwards. I am not really proud of this event, but it was a big wake-up call that set me back on the path of better behavior for the rest of my high school and college years.

ARCHDIOCESE OF SAN FRANCISCO

Saint Cecilia _____ School

San Francisco _____, Calif.

Report of __ Francis Dunnigan __ #9

Grade __ 3 __ Year 19 60 19 61

NOTE: PARENTS ARE INVITED TO DISCUSS THIS REPORT CARD WITH THE TEACHER AT THEIR EARLIEST CONVENIENCE, ESPECIALLY IF THE SCHOOL MARKS OR GROWTH IN DESIRABLE HABITS AND ATTITUDES ARE UNSATISFACTORY.

	First Report	Second Report	Third Report	Term Average	Fourth Report	Fifth Report	Sixth Report	Term Average
Religion	A+	A	A+		A+	A+	A-	
Social Studies	B	B	B		B+	A-	A-	
Reading	B	B-	C+		B	A-	A-	
Written English	B-	B-	B-		A	A	B+	
Oral English	B	B	B		B+	B+	A	
Spelling	B+	B+	A-		B+	A-	A	
Arithmetic	B+	B-	B+		B+	A-	A	
School Music	B-	B-	B-		B-	B-	B	
Art	C+	C+	C+		B+	C+	B	
Physical Ed.	C+	C+	C		C	C+	B	
Health and Safety	B	B	B		B	B	B	
Handwriting	C+	B-	B		C+	B	B+	
Science	B	B-	B		B	B	B+	
Times Tardy								
School Days Absent		2		1/2				
Deportment	B+	A-	A-		A-	A-	A	
Courtesy	B	B+	A+		A-	A-	A	
Application	B	B-	B		B+	A-	A	
Promotion Doubtful								

Sister Michael Marian
(Teacher

A Excellent, 95-100   B Good, 85-94   C Average, 75-84
D Not up to grade   F Failure

From the mid-1940s through the mid-1970s, report cards were distributed to each student at the front of the classroom by Monsignor Collins, who paid particular attention to the letter grades in religion and in the "below the line" categories of deportment, courtesy and application. *Author's collection.*

The Sisters of the Holy Names assigned to St. Cecilia School in 1960–61, photographed in the walled garden of the convent. *Standing, from left to right*: Sister Joseph Miriam, Sister Michael Marion, Sister Miriam Thomas, Sister Mary Noella, Sister M. Virginia Therese, Sister Madeleine Rita, Sister Michaeline Mary, Sister Ann Mary and Sister Miriam Bernardine. *Seated, from left to right*: Sister M. Joseph Anthony, Sister Andrew Marie, Sister Guadalupe Maria, Sister M. Patricia Rose and Sister Mary Eucharista. *Courtesy Archives of the Sisters of the Holy Names of Jesus and Mary, U.S.–Ontario Province.*

CECILIAN CLUB
ST. CECILIA'S PARISH
SAN FRANCISCO
THIS IS TO CERTIFY THAT

Alice Lynch _____SIGNATURE

IS AN ACTIVE MEMBER IN GOOD STANDING

REV. JOHN J. SCANLON
_____CHAPLAIN

OFFICERS
JOHN DOHERTY Pres.   BARBARA VERGA, Vice Pres.
JERRY KELLEHER, Treas.   JANET SPECKMAN, Sec'y.
NANCY MALLEY) Sgt. at Arms
PHIL McGUIRE)

NO. 172

A teen club membership card, 1950s. *Courtesy Mibach family.*

✠ *All Married Couples* ✠

are invited to

A Cana Conference

at

ST. CECILIA'S

1:30 P.M. - MARCH 10

___

THEME: Marriage—Your Road to Happiness

SPEAKERS: Priest and Doctor

TOPICS:
- Marriage—Your Vocation
- Unity—The Key to Happiness
- The Challenge of a Christian Marriage
- God's Plan for Marriage

___

This Cana Conference Is Presented for

Married Couples of All Ages.

___

please make a reservation by phoning
LO 6-8588 or SE 1-5438

Left: Realizing the importance of the institution of matrimony, the parish began offering a series of "Cana Conferences" to married couples beginning in the early 1960s. *Parish Archives.*

Below: Father Patrick Peyton's "Rosary Crusade" was held at the Polo Field of Golden Gate Park in October 1961, with a crowd estimated at more than 500,000 people at the peak of the event—the largest single gathering in the history of San Francisco. Monsignor Collins was especially pleased to note that the entire area around St. Cecilia Church was virtually deserted as he made his way to Golden Gate Park. *Courtesy St. Gabriel Parish Archives.*

PERSONAL REMINISCENCE: CATHY SMITH SAFFEL

My grandparents Fred and Kitty Wolfinger were original St. Cecilia parishioners. By 1920 or so, they had moved from 23rd Avenue into a new, larger home on 20th Avenue near Ulloa, just a few steps from Larsen Park. My mother missed attending St. Cecilia School because she was already in high school by 1930, when the parish school opened. For high school, she attended the old St. Rose Academy on Pine Street, which was run by the Dominican nuns. In those days, there was still a streetcar line that ran on 20th Avenue from Wawona to Lincoln Way. Since my mother was often the first passenger to be picked up in the morning or the last one dropped off in the afternoon, conductors used to stop right in front of the house for her, which she thought was a great treat. When I attended St. Cecilia School from 1949 to 1957, our family—consisting of my parents, my grandmother, my sister and myself, plus three brothers—still lived in that big house near the Park. Like my mother, I also went to St. Rose for high school (where I was known as a "Rosebud" because I was the daughter of a St. Rose grad), though the daily commute involved several buses, as the streetcar line along 20th Avenue had been removed in 1946. Some of my own children lived in that same house for several years after my grandmother and both of my parents were gone—more than seventy-five years of wonderful memories, mostly in the Monsignor Collins era of St. Cecilia Parish.

Surprise end-of-school-year party for a beloved teacher, Sister Ann Mary, given by her class, Grade 4/Room 17, in June 1962. *Author's collection.*

PERSONAL REMINISCENCE: MR. ROBERT DRUCKER

I was hired as a coach at St. Cecilia's in October 1962. My friend, Pete Murray, longtime coach at Holy Name of Jesus School, called me to tell me that there was an opening at SC. I had grown up on 24th Avenue in St. Anne's Parish, was just out of the army, going to USF and had expressed to Pete an interest in coaching. I was interviewed by the principal, Sister Michaeline Mary. She was a very nice person and very supportive of me. I was then interviewed by my mentor, Tony Laberrique, a San Francisco fireman and athletic director at St. Cecilia School, who recommended that I be hired. Father Ray Smith was my contact person at the rectory.

From 1962 to 1965, I coached two grades each of basketball and baseball until I was hired at SI in May 1965 by Father Carlin, SJ, and Father McFadden, SJ. I don't know if my time at SC had anything to do with my being hired at SI, but I don't think it hurt. My hiring certainly didn't have anything to do with my mediocre basketball career as a player at SI, although I relish my four years as a player and the teammates and friendships that I made there. I was appointed the basketball coach at SI in the spring of 1966, with just three years of CYO coaching experience.

My three years of coaching at SC were among the most important in my life journey. I coached many wonderful kids, met great families, developed spiritually and learned a lot about coaching and myself. Most importantly, it was clear that I loved coaching, although I also had an unexpressed desire to become a teacher as well. I couldn't see being one without the other. Tony Laberrique and the parents were unbelievably supportive of me, and that is something I will be eternally grateful for.

The most memorable story of Monsignor Collins was Sports Night in the auditorium. The guests: Willie Mays and Willie McCovey. Mays was living nearby, and Monsignor was trying to recruit Willie to send his son to SC. The event was preceded by a steak dinner at the rectory, and it was a great evening.

I am still married to Kathy Griffin Drucker—it will be fifty years in November 2016, and we have four children: Katie Drucker Kohmann, Molly Drucker Krauss, Joe Drucker (SI, '90) and Christina Drucker Luceno (SI, '93; first coed class at SI). We also have twelve grandchildren, including one SI grad, Kevin (class of 2015); two who are SI, class of 2017; and one still at St. Cecilia's.

So, life is good, and I consider myself a very lucky man.

In the late 1950s, the Sisters of Social Service, an order of nuns established in California in 1908, acquired a large home at the northeast corner of 20th Avenue and Ulloa Street for their new convent. Although their ministry took them throughout the city, the Sisters, clad in distinctive gray habits, were a regular presence at Mass at St. Cecilia Church.

The 1960s saw the commencement of the Second Vatican Council and a greater amount of public outreach by the Catholic Church worldwide. St. Cecilia parish offered "Inquiry Classes" for the public in order to explain Catholic traditions and beliefs. At the same time, the position of director of adult education was established in order to provide an introduction to Catholicism for adults who wished to convert.

In the fall of 1964, Monsignor Collins was pleased to announce that the remaining debt for construction of the new church was about to be paid off. In December of that year, a solemn ceremony was held to mark the new consecrated status of St. Cecilia Church. Twelve "consecration crosses" were added to the interior walls of the church, each holding a candle. Coming less than ten years after the new church was completed, there was tremendous cause for celebration. Just after the New Year's holiday, Monsignor Collins hosted a parish-wide banquet at the then new Hilton Hotel in downtown San Francisco to thank the parishioners and countless other donors who had brought the dream of a permanent church building to fruition.

On December 1, 1964, Monsignor Collins was also awarded a papal appointment from Pope Paul VI as Prothonotary (sometimes spelled Protonotary) Apostolic—a title of honor, seldom used today, that was bestowed on him in recognition of his many accomplishments.

ST. CECILIA SCHOOL UNIFORM REQUIREMENTS

1ST THROUGH 6TH GRADES

☐ Green plaid jumper of wool-orlon, 9.98 to 10.98
☐ Green plaid bolero jacket, 7.75 and 8.50
☐ Green orlon sweater, 4.98 and 5.98
☐ White dacron and cotton blouse with peter pan collar, 2.98
☐ Green half hat, 1.75
☐ White anklets
☐ White oxfords

7TH THROUGH 8TH GRADES

☐ Green plaid knife pleated skirt of wool and orlon, 9.98 to 10.98
☐ Bolero jacket, 8.50
☐ Green orlon sweater, 7.98
☐ White dacron and cotton blouse with peter pan collar, 3.98
☐ Green half hat, 1.75
☐ White anklets
☐ White oxfords
All prices subject to change

City of Paris School Uniforms, Third Floor

City of Paris department store advertisement for St. Cecilia School girls' uniforms, 1963. *Courtesy Mary Landers.*

All Welcome

Catholics and non-Catholics

A friendly explanation
of Catholic teachings

Answers to your questions

No Fees   No Obligations

SAINT CECILIA'S PARISH
Announces
an

INQUIRY
CLASS

to be conducted by

FATHER CORNELIUS BURNS

Every Monday evening
at 7:30

Starting October 7, 1963

SAINT CECILIA'S LOWER CHURCH
17th Avenue and Vicente Street

In 1963, St. Cecilia Church began conducting public outreach programs to explain Catholic beliefs to all in the community. This program eventually led to the hiring of an adult education coordinator for the parish in 1965. *Parish Archives.*

SAINT CECILIA'S RECTORY
2555 SEVENTEENTH AVENUE
SAN FRANCISCO 16, CALIFORNIA

FROM THE OFFICE OF THE PASTOR

November 30, 1964

Mr. and Mrs. Thomas F. Landers
2477 - 14th Avenue
San Francisco, California

Dear Mr. and Mrs. Landers:

I wish to extend to you a most cordial invitation to be my Guest at a Parish Banquet on Sunday, January 3rd, 1965 in the Grand Ball Room of the new Hilton Hotel at Mason and O'Farrell Streets, San Francisco. There will be a No Host Cocktail Party beginning at Five O'Clock on the Second Floor, adjacent to the Grand Ball Room. Dinner will be served promptly at Six O'Clock. Since we have 5000 Adult Parishioners, but have room for only 2000 in the Grand Ball Room, I request that you kindly return the enclosed card before December 10th if you will be able to attend.

The purpose of this Banquet is twofold:
First, to celebrate three great events in the life of our Parish, namely:

1) The Solemn Consecration of our Church of Saint Cecilia on Friday, December 18, 1964;
2) The "Paying Off our Debt" on our beautiful "House of God" on December 31st, 1964; and
3) The inauguration of our new "Apostolic Program"---specifically, the inauguration of our Convert Program on January 1st, 1965, under the leadership of Mr. William Parrott, Director of Adult Education in our Parish.

The Second Purpose of this Banquet is to express to you my sincere and heartfelt thanks and gratitude for your loyalty, your cooperation, your support and your generosity. Saint Cecilia Church---"Our Beautiful House of God"---now solemnly consecrated to Almighty God and now free of all debt stands today and will always stand as a monument of your Faith in and Love of God and as a monument of your cooperation and generosity.

Thanking you again and praying upon you every blessing, I am

Faithfully yours,

Harold E. Collins

Right Reverend Harold E. Collins
Pastor

The December 1964 consecration of St. Cecilia Church celebrated the retirement of the remaining financial debt—a significant goal for the parish just ten years after construction commenced on the new church. Monsignor Collins was pleased to host a celebratory banquet in January 1965 to mark the milestone. *Courtesy Mary Landers.*

PERSONAL REMINISCENCE: FRED WALSH

In 1963, my parents, along with my two sisters, Loretta and Amy, brother Mike and myself, all moved from an apartment at Parkmerced to a home on 18th Avenue near Vicente. I was still enrolled at St. Thomas More School, but my parents were hoping that I could be accepted at St. Cecilia, as we lived less than two hundred feet away from the school building. Originally, I was not allowed to transfer in, since the sixth grade was already beyond its capacity of fifty students per classroom at the time. One day early in the school year, I was playing basketball in the schoolyard on a Friday afternoon, and another boy about my age told me that he was leaving the school because his father had been transferred to a new city and their whole family was moving away. I immediately took him with me to the convent, rang the doorbell and spoke with Sister Michaeline Mary, who was the school's principal at the time. Over the weekend, she called and spoke with my parents, and on the following Monday morning in September of 1963, I joined the class of 1966 in sixth grade and spent three enjoyable years with them before going on to Riordan High School. I'm now retired from a forty-year career in the San Francisco Fire Department, living with my wife in Santa Rosa and still in touch with many of my St. Cecilia classmates as we celebrate our Golden Diploma reunion. Mom [Margaret Walsh] continued living in the same home for well over forty years and became one of the first lay Eucharistic ministers, bringing Holy Communion to her housebound neighbors until she was well past the age of 90—and before celebrating her 100th birthday at Little Sisters on Lake Street—so St. Cecilia Parish remains an important chapter in the story of our family.

ST. CECILIA PARISH IN THE NEWS

In 1966, there was a mid-decade statewide redistricting of Senate, Assembly and Congressional seats in California, as power began shifting to more heavily populated areas. San Francisco, for example, which once had many more representatives in the various legislative bodies than it has today, had to acknowledge the population growth of other counties, particularly those located in Southern California. With a fixed number of legislative seats available, that meant that boundaries would have to be *completely redrawn for the entire state. Throughout the process, Monsignor Collins was a strong advocate for the political unity of St. Cecilia Parish. Backed by the support of Nineteenth Assembly District member Charlie Meyers—a nearby resident who, for years, was a fixture at every wake and rosary on the west side of town— St. Cecilia Parish had legislative boundaries drawn around it and never through it, with Meyers insisting on the use of parish boundary lines rather than census tracts when determining new legislative districts. Monsignor Collins was adamant that his parish would never be divided into two by an arbitrary line, in the same manner that Interstate 280 had recently divided and destroyed the community spirit of nearby St. Michael Parish.*

Courtesy Paul Rosenberg, San Francisco political observer.

By the late 1960s, the Holy Names Sisters at St. Cecilia School had begun the clothing transition to "interim" habits of navy blue, with short veils, as shown on Sister Sylvia Bartheld. By the 1980s, most of the Sisters had transitioned to "civilian"-style clothing. *Ring family photo.*

Personal Reminiscence: Claire Mibach Fugate

I walked through the doors of St. Cecilia School for the first time at an open house for new students in the fall of 1962, along with my extended family: my parents, Richard and Jane Mibach; my grandmother Hazel Mibach; my brother, Brian; and my grandfather's cousin Joseph Mibach (SFFD) and his wife, my Aunt Agnes. As we walked down the first-floor hallway, my grandmother pointed out the graduation photos of my father, my Aunt Rita Mibach Smith and my uncle Warren (Chubby) Mibach. Proudly steeped in Catholic tradition, the Mibach family was delighted that I would be the standard bearer for the next generation.

On my first day of school, I was a bit frightened and was comforted by my grandmother's assurance that my guardian angel was always with me. Heading out to recess, I proudly pointed out my family members' photos to classmates, only to be sternly informed by Sister M. Rose Philomena that "there is no talking in the hallway." I knew at that moment that I'd felt the brush of an angel's wing.

My parents' home was in the West Portal area, and on many Mondays, I was sent to school with an orchid corsage that one of the Mibach women had worn on the prior Saturday night. I reverently placed the flower at the foot of the statue of Mary in the school's first-floor hallway opposite Grade 3, Room 9.

My family was very active in parish life: Grandma Hazel was the first treasurer of the Women's Guild at St. Cecilia School, and my grandfather Bertram was active in the Men's Club. Uncle Joe was a Sunday usher, and for decades, Aunt Agnes was the sacristan who maintained the altar. All the Mibach women belonged to the League of the Sacred Heart, and my dad, uncle and their cousins were all altar servers. The Mibach boys often told the story of why they always signed up for the 6:30 a.m. daily Mass—it seems that afterward they received a delicious free breakfast from the housekeeper at the rectory.

My St. Cecilia class of 1970 recently celebrated our forty-fifth reunion. We all fondly remembered the Sunday Children's Mass, May procession, Stations of the Cross and Benediction of the Blessed Sacrament. It was generally agreed there was a lot of incense used in those days. Smiles and tears appeared as we remembered the parish picnics, sno-cone days, annual festival and ham dinner in the Cafeteria (ham, mashed potatoes, sauerkraut), spaghetti shuffle dinners, CYO sports, annual Holy Name tournament, dancing class with Mrs. Hunter and field trips. Sadly, we recalled pivotal national events that occurred, such as the assassination of President Kennedy during the fall of our second-grade year in 1963.

Many members of the Mibach family have moved on from this world to the next; however, I do know that they still watch over the family because every once in a while I see or feel the brush of an angel's wing and remember Grandma's words from so long ago.

SAINT CECILIA RECTORY
2555 SEVENTEENTH AVENUE
SAN FRANCISCO, CALIFORNIA 94116

FROM THE OFFICE OF THE PASTOR

June 5, 1974

Dear Parents:

As we approach the close of this School year, I think back to the many boys and girls who have graduated from our School of St. Cecilia. I think of those who have gone on to serve Our Lord as Priests and Sisters, and the many more who serve Him in Christian Marriage.

I think too of all those who have sacrificed a great deal that all this could come true. I think of you wonderful parents and of all that you have been doing in your turn to give your children the best of Catholic education.

So it is with great reluctance that I write to you today, but write I must.

Four years ago it was necessary to raise the tuition in our School in order to allay rising deficits. I had hoped that it would not be necessary to do so again for some time. But now I find that in order to keep the School deficit at a reasonable level, and, more importantly, to insure the continued high quality of Catholic education for your children, it is necessary to increase the tuition rates.

Effective September 1, 1974, the new rates will be:

For those living in the Parish	For those outside the Parish
One child . . . . . $30 per month	One Child . . . . . . $40 per month
Two children . . . $45 per month	Two Children . . . . $55 per month
Three children or more .$50 per month	Three Children . . . $60 per month

It should be noted that these rates represent an attempt at meeting the rapidly rising costs of education. Even with these increases we will still show a deficit in excess of $50,000 for the coming year. I can only hope another increase will not be necessary in the near future, because I fully recognize how much you are already sacrificing in time and money.

Tuition alone has never paid for the operation of our Catholic School system either here or any place else. In our Parish we are extremely fortunate to have many people who feel grateful for their own Catholic education and who assist you by way of our monthly School Collection. I thank them and I thank you who have continued to respond so generously to this First Sunday Collection. I would only urge those of you who haven't given to please do what you can. Even a little bit is better than nothing.

Now, there may be some for whom this increase may prove to be too much. All I can say is no child has ever been or will be turned away from St. Cecilia School for financial reasons. If you find the burden too heavy, then please see me or one of my Assistant Priests, and suitable arrangements will be made.

Once again, thank you for all you have been doing for your children and for letting us be a part of it.

Praying upon you every blessing, I am

Faithfully yours,

Harold E. Collins

Readers can literally feel the pain that Monsignor Collins felt in 1974 when he had to announce a significant tuition increase for the coming school year. Although the level of tuition was quite modest by today's standards, the increasing costs of running a private school in the late twentieth century were becoming increasingly apparent to everyone. *Courtesy Phil and Helen Murphy.*

Right: By the 1974–75 school year, class size was declining rapidly in the lower grades, reflecting both new archdiocesan guidelines and also reduced birthrates from the late 1960s. Within a few years, this shift allowed for the reopening of kindergarten. *Courtesy McKeon family.*

Below: Mrs. Margaret Carberry, longtime school secretary, in her office, 1976. *Parish Archives.*

Tripping the Light Fantastic: Remembering Inez Hunter

This article by Jo Anne Quinn first appeared on the website of the Western Neighborhoods Project in January 2010 (http://www.outsidelands.org/mrs-hunter.php). It is reprinted here with permission.

Many a local boy recalls being forced to dance with GIRLS (ewww... cooties!!) during the weekly classes led by Mrs. Inez Hunter at a number of Catholic grade schools in the Sunset and Richmond Districts.

Our teacher was born Inez Alma Beirne on November 15, 1902, the daughter of Raymond Beirne and Florence Eisfelder Beirne, both of California. She graduated from San Francisco's Girl's High School in 1920.

She married Thomas "Jack" Hunter. Mrs. Hunter was a real character and her husband was like-minded...a big man with a hearty laugh and a deep, scratchy voice, who always sported a HUGE cigar. They were a perfectly matched couple.

She had two daughters, Nancyhelen and Carol Inez (now known as Rabia) and saw Nancyhelen go on to be a major feminist force in Washington State in the area of encouraging women to run for political office. Nancyhelen passed away on December 1, 2008, at the age of 77. Rabia, now 74, is currently an Advisory Council Member for the Sonoma County Council Committee on Aging.

Why and how Mrs. Hunter decided to become involved in the art of dance is not known. Aside from teaching in Catholic schools, she also had a dance studio that she operated out of her own home, teaching ballet, tap, jazz and acrobatics. Your author was one of her students. She gave recitals at places like the Laguna Honda Home and the San Francisco Maritime Museum, usually during the holiday seasons. They were always great fun, despite the grueling rehearsals, mothers laboriously sewing elaborate costumes and dads building props.

In 1985, the St. Cecilia class of 1960 invited Mrs. Hunter, along with our other teachers, to a 25th reunion held in the school's auditorium. She did not hesitate, just like in the "old days," to pick out the tallest boy to engage in an honorary dance. She also danced with a few of the girls, just to make sure they had remembered their long-ago lessons. Seeing this wonderful woman again, after so many years, added a welcomed and whimsical touch to the gathering.

On the occasion of her 85th birthday, she threw a big party at a hotel in San Francisco and invited not only friends and family but also former students. The turnout was impressive. Everyone brought old photos of their dance school days, which were pinned up on a bulletin board next to Mrs. Hunter's contributions. Her husband, with his ever-present large cigar, delighted in being surrounded by such an enthusiastic group. Mrs. Hunter even did a little dance for us. By golly, she still had all the right moves…

Two contributors to Western Neighborhoods Project's message boards also remembered Mrs. Hunter thusly:

PAUL JUDGE: Over in the Outer Richmond, Inez Hunter provided folk dancing lessons to every 1st through 8th grade on Tuesday mornings at St. Thomas the Apostle. She was regularly outfitted in one of her colorful folk dresses and soft dance shoes. She impressed me with how effortlessly and gracefully she glided across the floor. She worked pretty hard to teach us and didn't truck resistance—thus we ended up being able to dance. It was nearly obligatory for us boys to decline interest or outward enthusiasm to this weekly task. I don't know how the girls felt, but it sure beat spending time at the chalkboard perpetually diagramming sentences. Like many youngsters in the neighborhood, my younger sister Mary took ballet lessons from Mrs. Hunter at her studio in the garage of a home near 45th and Cabrillo. It wasn't unusual to see grade school girls, dressed in their tights, toting toe shoes and making their way to afternoon dance lessons while us boys played ball in the street.

WILL MCCULLAR: I went to St. Cecilia from 1st grade through 4th grade (1961–64). I remember dance classes with Mrs. Hunter. Because I was tall for my age, she always made me dance with her as my partner. It made me a better dancer.

One of her female students recalled, "Mrs. Hunter was a godsend to me after my Mom died. Don't know what I would have done without her! Even though I quit ballet eventually, I still kept in touch with her. We went out to dinner quite frequently as she always wanted to eat somewhere that she couldn't go to on her own after her husband died. Because I could drive, we went to places all over San Francisco. And she was in pretty good health until she got cancer in one of her feet (isn't that ironic since she taught dancing). She went downhill pretty fast after that, and ended up with pneumonia."

Homily at funeral of Msgr. Collins

'The Symphony is finished . . .'

The following is the full text of the homily delivered by Archbishop John R. Quinn at the Mass of Christian Burial for Monsignor Harold E. Collins, Pastor Emeritus of St. Cecilia's, San Francisco, on Friday, December 19, 1980.

• • •

One of the great and best loved works of music is the *Unfinished Symphony.* While all symphonies have three movements, the *Unfinished* has only two.

The third and final movement was never written and the masterpiece stands incomplete.

Today as we come to celebrate this Mass of his burial, it seems to me that Monsignor Collins' life is not unlike the *Unfinished Symphony.*

The first movement of his life's symphony is Psalm 42. Like almost all boys who become priests, Harold Collins' earliest memories were of serving Mass.

In order to qualify for that great honor, he had to memorize the ancient Latin words which the altar boys said in dialog with the priest at the beginning of Mass.

And the very first words, which he was then to say each day for the greater part of his life, were these: "I will go unto the altar of God. To God who is the joy of my youth."

For all who knew him it was clear that for Harold Collins the most prized possession of his life was the priesthood.

And it is also significant that the words of the psalm were composed by David in the evening of his life and in a time of personal anguish.

And so it was ever with Monsignor Collins: faithfully going up to the altar of God, to God the joy of his youth, and of his age.

And amid all the great honors and responsibilities that came to him through his long life, there was never anything more treas-

ured and more precious, nothing of which he was prouder, than that gift which the love of God gave to him on that June morning in 1925 when Archbishop Hanna ordained him a priest forever.

So great and so strong was that grace in him that he rightly claimed something of a record in the number of young men whom he sent to the seminary and whom he lovingly referred to as "the priestly sons," and whose pictures covered the walls of his room.

Indelible in his mind, too, was the sacred promise of reverence and obedience made to the Bishop on the solemn day of his ordination, and he often spoke of this.

His whole life was built in childlike simplicity and faith around that vow and in living it faithfully he found strength, joy and peace because like Christ he sought not his own will but the will of Him in whom alone is our peace.

The second movement of the symphony is Psalm 26. This psalm, too, was on his lips each day for the greater part of his life.

And beginning at its sixth verse are these words: "I will wash my hands among the innocent and will go around your altar, O Lord, that I may hear the voice of your praise and tell of all Your wondrous works. I have loved, O Lord, the beauty of Your house and the place where Your glory dwells."

This Church of St. Cecilia is the enduring witness of those words. Like that great exponent of poverty, the Curé of Ars, Monsignor Collins rightly believed that anything used for divine worship should be beautiful, inspiring and uplifting.

But he also loved the beauty of God's house in the human heart. He loved his parishioners and above all he loved the children.

He spoke to them about God and taught them, too, to love the beauty of God's house. A grown man and woman of St. Cecilia's parish can remember in childhood stepping into the Church for a visit after school and finding Monsignor Collins kneeling before the Blessed Sacrament making his daily hour of prayer.

And those who know him well tell us that the substance of his prayer was "Lord, You have sent me here. Now help me to do something for You and for Your people."

And now the long day of his earthly life has closed. But the symphony no longer remains unfinished. At last there is the third and final movement.

How often he loved to tell the stories of Archbishop Mitty. And how many times did he walk down the aisle with the Archbishop on the great occasions in St. Mary's Cathedral. And as the Archbishop entered, the choir would sing "Ecce Sacerdos Magnus."

And this now becomes the third movement of the symphony and it final and glorious resolution. But it is no longer of Archbishop Mitty that the song speaks now.

It is the Angel of Death who comes at evening time for Harold Collins, and grasping his hand lifts the veil of faith as he leads him from this world into eternity and places him before Christ, risen from the dead.

"Ecce Sacerdos Magnus," sings the angel. Here indeed is the great high priest "who has passed through the heavens, Jesus, the Son of God." (Heb. 4:14)

And so the once unfinished symphony becomes the unending symphony of love and peace. And as we say good-bye to "the finest, the greatest, and the best" we commend him to the mercy of God. May he rest in everlasting peace.

Our teacher pirouetted into the light of that Great Studio in the Sky on November 14, 1992, one day short of her ninetieth birthday and the big party her daughters had planned for her. We owe a huge vote of thanks to Inez Alma Beirne Hunter for trying to teach a bunch of awkward preadolescents how to be social and graceful. Perhaps she did not always succeed, but she left us with some wonderful memories and a few dance steps with which to impress our dates.

Top: Incoming pastor Monsignor James McKay and retiring pastor Monsignor Harold E. Collins in front of the rectory, 1976. Monsignor Collins was seldom seen without the magenta sash that distinguished him among the clergy. *Parish Archives.*

Left: The December 1980 funeral for Monsignor Collins was one of the largest in the history of the parish. As the hearse made its way to 19th Avenue for the final ride to Holy Cross Cemetery, more than a few in the crowd of mourners wiped away a tear and remarked, "We were lucky to have had him—we will not see his like again." From the *Monitor. Parish Archives.*

Monsignor Collins's retirement in December 1976 came exactly thirty years after his appointment as pastor. Much had been accomplished during those three decades, and the man responsible for the greatest changes in the history of St. Cecilia Parish was now in his late seventies and about to embark on a well-deserved retirement. Assuming the title Pastor Emeritus, he remained a presence in both the parish and in the neighborhood, living in the same modest room over the rectory's entrance—his only home since 1946.

Gradually, though, ill health began to intrude, limiting his activities to an occasional dinner gathering with family members and close friends. In 1980, he reluctantly gave up his room in the rectory for an increased level of care that was available at Nazareth House in San Rafael.

Monsignor Collins went to be with the Lord in December 1980, and his funeral, just a week before Christmas, was an occasion filled with joy for a life well lived, as well as a service of thanksgiving from the thousands of people who had benefitted from his wisdom and kindness over the years.

Streetwise: The Finest, the Greatest and the Best

The following piece by Frank Dunnigan was originally written in December 2010 for the author's monthly "Streetwise" column, published by the Western Neighborhoods Project (www.outsidelands.org). It marked the thirtieth anniversary of the passing of Monsignor Collins.

Many people said that if Harold Collins hadn't become a priest, he would have been the best governor California could ever have hoped for, since he knew how to raise money, make people work together and still enjoy life—all at the same time. Now that he has been gone for thirty years—exactly the same amount of time that he spent as pastor of St. Cecilia's—it's time to reflect on what made this remarkable man such a memorable part of so many lives in the Outside Lands.

Born in San Francisco's Mission District on August 17, 1899, Harold E. Collins was ordained a priest at the old St. Mary's Cathedral on Van Ness Avenue in June of 1925, and he covered a variety of assignments in his early years, including brief teaching stints at both St. Ignatius and Sacred Heart High Schools during the Depression years. Even before his arrival at St. Cecilia's, he was well known in San Francisco's religious community as Secretary to Archbishop Mitty from 1939 to 1946, as well as for his authorship of a detailed reference book, *The Church: Its Edifice and Appointments*, which, for decades, was the definitive work on ecclesiastical architecture throughout the United States.

Monsignor, as he preferred to be known, arrived at St. Cecilia's four days after Christmas of 1946 to find a quiet, middle-class parish with not much going on. He knew intuitively that change was coming fast, as GIs were returning home en masse to settle down, buy homes and raise families.

Upon seeing the crowded conditions at Sunday Mass, he immediately went to work to have the sand lot at the NW corner of 17th Avenue and Vicente Street paved and used for parking, in order to accommodate the increasing number of automobiles that were appearing following the conclusion of the war years. As homes continued to be built on the remaining sand dunes in the neighborhood, he also remodeled the hall under that old church into a "lower church" in order to increase seating capacity and better serve his new congregation.

Also sensing the advancing age of some of his parishioners—the "50-plus crowd" he once called them after he himself had become a member—he made the simple change of adding a couple of sturdy concrete benches to the entrance to the old 17th Avenue church building so that those senior members of the community could have a seat while waiting to picked up by younger family members after Sunday Mass—something that Grandma Dunnigan thoroughly enjoyed before the new church was built in 1956 when Dad would pick her up after the 12:15 p.m. Mass for the ride back uphill to her home on 21st Avenue between Quintara and Rivera.

One small idea that Monsignor implemented upon becoming pastor was highly indicative of his future successes. For years, it had been the practice at St. Cecilia's and elsewhere to allow worshippers to make change for paper currency and 50-cent pieces by distributing a plate full of quarters, dimes and nickels prior to the passing of the collection basket. Monsignor decided to help increase the collection by insisting from the pulpit that he wanted a "silent" collection—that is, currency only, with no coins—or that he was looking forward to a "green" Christmas. His gentle reminders spurred everyone to be more generous as the Depression and the austere war years began to fade from memory.

Parishioners expressed immediate satisfaction for the changes that they saw, and Monsignor himself was proud that the various construction projects had been accomplished in the past at the least possible cost. He knew that he was about to embark on an expansion—in fact, a doubling of size—of the modest eight-classroom school building, in order to cope with the baby boom that he knew was already underway—Sunday baptisms in the postwar years were running far ahead of anything previously experienced.

Almost overnight, he achieved this goal, and by February of 1948, a mere fourteen months after his arrival, the archbishop was presiding over the dedication of an expanded school building that included eight additional classrooms (allowing for two classes at each grade level, and accommodating 50+ students apiece during the boom years of the 1950s and 1960s), plus space for both morning and afternoon kindergarten classes. That project also included a renovated cafeteria, plus a large auditorium at the basement level, both of which continue to sustain heavy use (the cafeteria now housing the kindergarten following the conversion of the original kindergarten space to music) more than sixty years later. The students were his "little pigeons," and it was clear that Monsignor's primary focus was the support and development of the children of his parish.

By the early 1950s, the postwar growth of the parish was well underway. Monsignor's next project was his most ambitious ever, and it was one that had eluded both of his predecessors: that of constructing a permanent church building that would be large enough to serve the community adequately into the future, thus relieving the overcrowded conditions that still existed every Sunday morning in both the upper and lower portions of the existing church. That old "temporary" church, just north of the present rectory and facing 17th Avenue, had been serving the parish for decades, first as a parish hall on Taraval Street in the World War I era and then moved to its new site and renovated into a church in the late 1920s and expanded in 1947.

When it came time to raise money for the construction of the present church, circa 1952–53, Monsignor demonstrated his phenomenal fundraising skills by asking everyone in the parish to pledge a certain amount, payable over a few years. Then, understanding human nature and peer pressure only too well, Monsignor had a group of parish ladies type up 3x5 file cards with each household's name, address AND DOLLAR AMOUNT PLEDGED and then posted these cards on bulletin boards in the vestibule of the church. There was practically a mob scene, as parishioners gathered around to see what the neighbors were giving. "Any of you who might like to increase your pledge, just call me—my door is always open to you," he said innocently. His phone rang off the hook as people called in to increase their donations to far more generous amounts. When ground was broken in May 1954, there was Monsignor, complete with his usual black cassock and magenta sash, wearing a hard hat and taking the controls in the cab of the first steam shovel to appear at the site—a bit of showmanship that he had borrowed from one of his idols, the late San Francisco mayor Sunny Jim Rolph.

Again, Monsignor's architectural knowledge led to the design of a magnificent structure that was more than double the capacity of old church, while still respecting the style and character of the neighborhood. Based on the hilly terrain, he also designed a new "lower church" as well, one that could be used for overflow attendance on Sundays and holy days. With a wall-to-wall drapery drawn across the sanctuary, it could also serve the parish as additional auditorium space.

Again, with a nod to his "senior" constituents, the new church was designed with an ambulatory entrance on 17th Avenue. "The only church building in San Francisco which can be entered without climbing a single step," he proudly announced. Another small point that was appreciated by many was the installation of electronic hearing aids in the confessionals. As Monsignor insisted, only partly tongue-in-cheek, "No one wants to have the neighbors hear what they are confessing, since in most cases, the neighbors usually know all about it."

In addition to creating a space conducive to worship, Monsignor also insisted on a few creature comforts, including daylight and fresh air. Putting aside the gloomy interiors of most churches, he designed the requisite stained-glass windows with religious scenes depicted in magnificently colored center ovals that were surrounded by lighter pastel-colored glass panels that allowed more daylight into the building. Further increasing the comfort of worshipers, he also insisted on multiple ground-level windows, depicting various saints, all of which could be opened easily to provide better air circulation.

Insisting that all parishioners hear the same sermon on Sundays, even with Mass being offered in two separate locations, the main level and the lower church, Monsignor designed the sound system in a way that the homily being delivered in the upper church was simultaneously broadcast in the lower church. Even though a different priest was saying Mass in each location, Monsignor firmly told them to coordinate the pace of the liturgy, and they did so, week after week, so that when the priest in the lower church pressed the speaker button, there was smooth transition as the sermon being given in the upper church was electronically piped into the lower church.

In the mid-1950s, just as the new steel frame was rising from the sand dunes, Monsignor managed to save the entire neighborhood from the blight and devastation of the planned Western Freeway (essentially eight elevated lanes of concrete in a straight line from SFO to the Golden Gate Bridge) by leaning hard on politicians, Democrats and Republicans alike. Over drinks and dinner (including desserts supplied by his favorite spot, the late, great Blum's), he made all of them see the wisdom of his point of view. His persuasion always managed to include a gentle reminder of how the thousands of parishioners in St. Cecilia Parish and the power of the pulpit might somehow adversely affect reelection prospects for all of them. (See the "Streetwise" column of January 2009, "Dad and Bill's Night Out," for more details on what the politicians had once planned for the neighborhood.) Thanks to the influence of Monsignor Collins, the Western Freeway was deader than the proverbial doornail, and the new church was formally dedicated in May of 1956 to much fanfare.

It was also at this time that the school's population began to exceed its Fire Department–sanctioned capacity of 800 students. When the expansion was completed in 1948, there were about 45 students in each of the 16 classrooms. With a double kindergarten class (morning and afternoon sessions of about 35 students each), the school population neared its ultimate capacity. By the fall of 1957, with most classes at 50 students each, the school was seriously overcrowded, and the difficult decision had to be made to close down the kindergarten. Ultimately, many of us born in the 1950s were enrolled in public schools for kindergarten, with the majority of us attending Parkside or West Portal Schools, before transitioning back in to St. Cecilia School for the start of first grade.

Ironically, there was a move underway in California in the late 1950s to rescind the tax-exempt status of private schools (granted by the state legislature just a few years earlier) with a ballot referendum that was eventually put before the voters in 1958. There was an ecumenical movement, particularly in San Francisco, in which the leaders of parochial schools, private schools and schools operated by other religious denominations banded together to urge the public to vote no on this potentially disastrous concept. Whether the closure of the St. Cecilia School kindergarten was purely related to fire safety or whether it also served as a subtle reminder to the public about the false economy of taxing private schools, the move achieved both goals. Voters went to the polls on Tuesday, November 4, 1958, and defeated the measure, known as Proposition 16, with a 70 percent "No" vote.

When the archdiocese was raising funds to build a new St. Mary's Cathedral after the 1962 arson fire, Monsignor again used the same technique involving 3x5 file cards posted with each family's pledge amount and then proudly announced that the generous parishioners of St. Cecilia's—"the finest, the greatest, and the best"—had contributed more to the cathedral building fund than any other parish in San Francisco.

The final debt on the new St. Cecilia's Church was paid off in January of 1965, incredibly, only nine years after its opening. Monsignor hosted a parish-wide banquet at the then-new Hilton Hotel and set a scroll "mortgage" on fire with a flaming sword in a dramatic bit of showmanship that remains unrivaled in the history of fundraising by any house of worship in San Francisco.

For more than thirty years, until his 1976 retirement, Monsignor distributed report cards to every grammar school student once every six weeks (and with fifty students per classroom—800 total—that was nearly 5,000 report cards per year). Most of the comments were standard: "beautiful," "very nice," "good" or "fine improvement." Anything less than a "B" in Religion or in any of the "below the line" categories—"Deportment," "Courtesy" or "Application"—was met with a cold stare. "What's this?" or "What happened here?" He was equally ruthless with families whose public school children failed to attend the weekly religious instruction classes in which they were enrolled. "We haven't been seeing your sister at CCD class lately—has she been sick?" Monsignor might ask a startled fifth grader. He knew the motto "It takes a village..." long before anyone else did.

Likewise, he came down hard on engaged couples who did not attend Mass regularly: "Do I know you? Let me see you at Mass every Sunday for a few months, and then we can sit down and talk about your wedding. I'm not running a social hall here, you know." Yet at the same time, he knew his audience well enough to announce sports scores from the pulpit as the 12:15 p.m. Mass was coming to an end just after 1:00 p.m., so that the congregation would not bolt for the doors before the final hymn: "Giants 2, Dodgers 1, bottom of the second..."

He also exerted a subtle influence on neighborhood morals in much the same way. When Reis' Pharmacy at 18th and Taraval began stocking *Playboy* magazine in the early 1960s, Monsignor urged his parishioners from the pulpit to "be sure and telephone my good friends the Reis Brothers and tell them what you think of their new selection of magazines." By Monday morning, the store had received hundreds of phone calls, and the offending periodicals were gone from the shelves before the students from St. Cecilia School were on their way home that afternoon.

Monsignor's heyday was the early 1960s, and the parish's nickname of "Harold's Club," after the South Lake Tahoe party spot, was fitting. John F. Kennedy was in place as the first Irish Catholic president of the United States; Pat Brown was the Irish Catholic governor of California (and a

St. Cecilia's parishioner as well); and by November of 1963, Jack Shelley had just become the Irish Catholic mayor-elect of San Francisco. (Other politicos in the parish included State Senator Gene McAteer, along with members of the San Francisco Board of Supervisors, Leo McCarthy and George Moscone.) When Pat and Bernice Brown came down to Sunday Mass at St. Cecilia's from their home in Forest Hill, they would try to slip in and out of church unobtrusively, but Monsignor always spotted them in the crowd (some said he was constantly "counting the house" in order to estimate the day's income from the collection plate), and he never missed the opportunity to announce from the pulpit, "Mr. Maestro, may we please have a little something for the Governor and the First Lady?" The organist and the choir would dutifully launch into a rousing version of "I Love You, California," with the entire congregation joining in. Years later, in 1996, the Brown family returned to St. Cecilia's for Pat's funeral—the largest single gathering of past, present and future politicians ever seen in the western neighborhoods.

Veteran city hall observer Paul Rosenberg, who is also a life member of San Francisco's venerable Irish-Israeli-Italian Society, recalls Monsignor Collins's impact on political redistricting efforts. "St. Cecilia's is the only parish in California that had its legislative boundaries drawn by the politicians to match the existing parish boundaries. Monsignor Collins insisted that his parish was NOT to be divided into two different legislative districts, thus diminishing the impact of parishioners' votes." He had ample cause to be concerned, for nearby St. Michael's Parish in the Oceanview–Merced Heights neighborhood was seriously impacted when the construction of Interstate 280 divided the parish into two distinct areas in the early 1960s. Such a fate would never befall St. Cecilia Parish while Monsignor Collins was in charge.

As the 1960s progressed and the political landscape changed due to elections, assassinations and general unrest, new faces found their way into office, but in 1967, Monsignor was on the bandwagon once again, this time to elect parishioner Gene McAteer as mayor. Yet the hand of fate was to intervene when a sudden heart attack on the Olympic Club's handball court ended the debonair candidate's life at age fifty-one, without warning, just prior to Memorial Day, thus resulting in an enormous funeral instead of a victory celebration. Today, a public high school for the arts stands as a memorial to Gene McAteer, while the tennis courts at nearby Sigmund Stern Grove were named for his wonderful wife, Frances, who was the longest-serving member of the city's Recreation and Park Commission.

Monsignor was open and forthright with his parishioners, offering a "State of the Parish" sermon every January. He could recall expenses better than any trained accountant. He knew exactly how much money had come in from the collection plate, school tuitions and bequests from deceased members of the parish. He knew precisely what had been paid out in staff salaries, water, PG&E, telephone, groceries, janitorial service and garbage collection. He spoke of how many baptisms, confirmations, weddings and funerals had taken place over the past year, along with how many families were registered in the parish, and what the total head count was for all of these households combined. He often closed with the gentle reminder, "Unless you've invented something that I don't know about, you can't take it with you," encouraging his audience to "Leave your money with me—I'll take better care of it than your children and grandchildren will." As a result, more than a few people have remembered St. Cecilia's very generously in their estate plans over the years. To this day, thirty full years after Monsignor's passing, the parish school continues to receive generous surprise bequests from the estates of elderly parishioners who remembered Monsignor's words and provided for posthumous donations via their written estate plans. [Author's 2016 update: The extensive exterior painting program that was recently undertaken was one of several parish projects funded via the very generous bequest of a home from the estate of a longtime parishioner.]

The Parish Festival, the school's primary fundraiser, used to coincide with Halloween each year, and Monsignor saw it as another chance to remind everyone that it was all about the children. For decades, he ran two festivals: a "Children's Festival" on Halloween Day and the regular festival on the weekend. It was easy enough to keep the same booths, while switching the prizes from goldfish in plastic bags and cupcakes to quarts of bourbon and chances to win a new car. From his deep pockets filled with dimes (and also his beloved jelly beans), Monsignor would toss out coins to the crowds of schoolchildren, knowing that they would certainly return with additional revenue from their parents and grandparents.

Monsignor wisely decided one year that the top prize in the raffle should not be a new car but rather cash. When questioned about the choice, he smilingly told his advisers that it was cheaper in the long run. "I might pay $2,000 for a car at dealer's cost, but when I hand out $2,000 in cash to someone, I know that I'm going get up to half of it back as a donation to the school!" And right he was. He often played the role of Jack Benny, reluctantly handing over the winnings in $100 bills, counting them out ever so slowly to some lucky winner, right there on the stage of the school's auditorium.

That person often felt just enough peer pressure from the audience to turn around on the spot and give a sizable chunk of the winnings right back to St. Cecilia School.

Monsignor loved wheeling and dealing in the world of finance and tooling around the neighborhood in a series of late-model Irish-green Oldsmobile 98s supplied by the long-gone C.M. Murphy dealership on 19th Avenue (and always outfitted with an "ah-*ooga*" horn, a slide whistle or a loud bell controlled by a floor button). Yet in spite of this, he kept those clear blue eyes focused on the people of his parish. Any family who suffered an unexpected job loss or death of the breadwinner was quietly assured not to worry about the school tuition for their children—a whopping six dollars per month per family back then—because "it has been taken care of." Likewise, Monsignor was not shy about notifying those in charge of various Catholic high schools if there was a difficult situation impacting any family in his parish and that some financial consideration on the part of the Jesuits or the Christian Brothers or the Sisters of Mercy would be most appreciated.

Understanding the financial diversity of the parish—the wealthy enclaves of Forest Hill and St. Francis Wood were represented, along with the teeming family-filled Sunset District, plus lots of elderly apartment-dwelling pensioners on fixed incomes—Monsignor was careful to mold his messages to fit all circumstances and all "customers." With politicians and corporate executives, he sounded fiscally conservative and almost Republican. With the rank-and-file, he expressed strong support for the working masses, sounding fiercely Democratic. With the elderly, he made it clear that he, too, was one of them, "born in the Mission District before the Fire." The rectory pointedly subscribed to both of San Francisco's two morning newspapers of the era: the *Examiner* (then Democratic-leaning) and the *Chronicle* (then Republican-leaning). When the parish held its memorable 1965 banquet, Monsignor shied away from the Republicanism of the St. Francis Hotel, as well as the Democratic leanings of philanthropist Ben Swig's Fairmont, for the "neutral" territory of the then new San Francisco Hilton. His comments from the pulpit over Labor Day weekend were always politically perfect statements: "We recognize and celebrate the contribution of all those who work for a living, be they labor or be they management."

At a time of uneasy racial transformation in the western neighborhoods, it was Monsignor Collins who set the tone by welcoming Terry Francois and his family when they became the first African Americans to purchase a home on nearby Taraval Street. While the elder Francois children continued to attend St. Anne School, the younger ones were enrolled at St. Cecilia.

Likewise, when Willie Mays and his wife experienced difficulty in purchasing a home in the area, Monsignor decided to throw a "Sports Night" in the school auditorium so that everyone could meet the Giants' slugger personally.

Further sensing the winds of social change, Monsignor hired the first Asian American teacher for St. Cecilia School in the early 1960s. There was also the inclusion of Spanish, French and "new math" in the school's curriculum at that time, which was unheard of in most other parishes, many of which were still separating their elementary school classes by gender—a practice that Monsignor never supported. He took a good deal of parental heat for some of the new curriculum components, but he understood where secondary education was heading, and he wanted all of us to be ready. Not surprisingly, though, he was also still a part of his generation and upbringing, and throughout his years as pastor, female teachers at St. Cecilia's were absolutely required to wear skirts or dresses; the few male teachers hired beginning in the late 1960s were told that they must always be attired in a coat and tie while in the classroom.

Every Sunday morning, he was front and center at the 9:00 a.m. "Children's Mass." With the student body seated by grade level, Monsignor focused on the first graders seated at the front, explaining to them exactly what was taking place during each part of the service. His daily involvement in the education of the school's children was an import part of his overall being. However, the question of whether he might occasionally have stepped on the toes of a nun whose grading policies were a bit too honest is a topic that may best be left unexplored.

For all his enthusiastic support of the children, however, many parents wondered why he was so adamantly opposed to constructing a gymnasium for school athletics on the property—an oft-repeated question in the 1960s. Fundraising would have been no problem, for Monsignor knew that drill perfectly. He acquiesced to the ongoing parental requests, but only with assurances that there were adequate basketball hoops and volleyball equipment in the school yard, plus upgraded night lighting, so that the children could play safely after dark. Pressed by his confidants to reconsider the idea of constructing a full-sized gymnasium on the property, he replied simply that he refused to take Sunday morning parking spaces away from "the paying customers" because that would negatively impact the financial base on which the school depended. In addition, the walled garden that he had constructed for the nuns in the late 1940s would have been jeopardized by the footprint of construction—and this was at a time when quiet reading and a brief respite from the rigors of the classroom were among the few small perks enjoyed by a convent full of religious women. Monsignor was not about to deprive them of this amenity. Indeed, the construction of the Durocher Pavilion in the new millennium required the removal of convent garden, but by that time, the population of nuns had decreased significantly, while those who were vowed religious at that time were able to engage in a variety of recreational activities that were not available to nuns decades earlier.

By the 1970s, Monsignor was forced to acknowledge the serious decline in the number of women entering religious life. He further noted that many of the laypeople being hired as teachers were unmarried career professionals, and thus, they did not have a spouse's union or government health plan and pension to fall back on. He was forced to abandon the standard paternalistic stance of the era: "They are doing the same work as the nuns, so why should they be paid more?" He struggled with the necessity of tuition increases because of the rising costs of operating an aging physical plant, plus the salary, health and retirement benefits for the ever-growing number of lay teachers who had begun to outnumber the nuns. These ongoing tuition increases, he feared, might place the cost of a Catholic school education beyond the means of many families. Although he was just beginning to grapple with this problem during his final years as pastor, there was no easy fix.

When he finally retired in 1976, Monsignor remained in residence on 17th Avenue as "Pastor Emeritus," still involved in tending to his flock. Ill health slowly began to take its toll, and his busy schedule was eventually reduced to an occasional Sunday night dinner out with family and close friends. In early 1980, he reluctantly gave up his room overlooking the schoolyard and spent his last few months living under the supervised care offered by Nazareth House in San Rafael.

At his pre-Christmas funeral in December 1980, the mood was joyous and grateful, a service of thanksgiving rather than one of grief. As Monsignor left his beloved church for the last time, more than one mourner wiped a tear away and gazed after him saying, "We'll not see his like again...." The hearse began its slow ride down Vicente Street and turned onto 19th Avenue, with a police escort all the way to Holy Cross Cemetery in Colma, as the organist and the choir continued to play the recessional "hymn" that was Monsignor's favorite, "The Beer Barrel Polka":

> There's a garden, what a garden,
> Only happy faces bloom there,
> And there's never any room there,
> For a worry, or a gloom there.

Oh, there's music, and there's dancing,
And a lot of sweet romancing,
When they play the polka,
They all get in the swing.
Every time they hear that oom-pah-pah,
Everybody feels so tra-lah-lah,
They want to throw their cares away,
They all go lah-de-ah-de-ay.
Then they hear a rumble on the floor, the floor,
It's the big surprise they're waiting for,
And all the couples form a ring,
For miles around you'll hear them sing...
Roll out the barrel,
We'll have a barrel of fun.
Roll out the barrel,
We've got the blues on the run.
Zing, boom, ta-ra-rel,
Ring out a song of good cheer,
Now's the time to roll the barrel,
For the gang's all here.

One month after Monsignor Collins's death, the parish established a most appropriate legacy, the Monsignor Collins School Fund, an endowed trust fund, set up in the same manner as similar funds at large eastern universities, that generates investment income to support the school's operations.

From 1980 until the end of the millennium, the fund grew to more than $1 million, and to well over $2 million today [now more than $3 million in 2016], with only the earnings being used to offset the ever-spiraling annual tuition costs. "Never touch principal" is the age-old advice of experienced financial counselors.

Thousands of children from homes throughout the Bay Area have passed through the halls of St. Cecilia School over the past thirty years, all of them benefitting from the work of Monsignor Collins and the generosity of countless previous donors to his fund.

This has become a fitting legacy, indeed, for a remarkable individual.

Chapter 5

THE MONSIGNOR MCKAY ERA

1976–1990

Monsignor Collins's retirement marked the return to St. Cecilia Parish of Father (later Monsignor) James P. McKay, who had served as a popular parish priest and assistant pastor in the 1950s and 1960s under Monsignor Collins's leadership. Between his two assignments at St. Cecilia Parish, Monsignor McKay held positions as the head of Catholic Cemeteries of the Archdiocese, as well as other pastoral assignments in the Bay Area, before his appointment as pastor of St. Cecilia Parish in July 1976.

Acknowledging that Monsignor Collins was "a hard act to follow," parishioners felt at home with Monsignor McKay because of his prior service at St. Cecilia, as well as his personable, take-charge approach. Monsignor McKay quickly took note of the fact that the parish population was aging. All of those World War II vets who had settled down to raise families in the late 1940s as the parish was expanding were now joining the ranks of retirees. Many younger people—lured by better weather, improved transit to the suburbs (BART began trans-bay service in the fall of 1972) and more affordable housing in other areas—began opting for homes outside San Francisco. Mass attendance was declining, as many parish households now had only one or two members, while school enrollment was off, as the last of the baby boomer generation (those born between 1946 and 1964) were set to graduate from elementary school in 1978.

These changes helped to bring about many improvements in parish life. The lower church, once a critical component in providing seating for the thousands and thousands of people who attended Sunday Mass at St.

Mrs. Catherine Ring and Miss Carolyn Daley, with a group of students in Mrs. Ring's classroom, Grade 2/Room 3, in February 1977. By this time, laywomen were making up a majority of the faculty at St. Cecilia School. *Parish Archives.*

Cecilia Church, could now be put to a new use. Renamed the Collins Center for the recently retired pastor, a new community was established there under the guidance of Sister Jeanne Cusick, SNJM, who had recently returned to the Bay Area from another assignment in order to help care for her own elderly father. Sister Jeanne soon established a number of programs for parish seniors: day trips, bingo, language lessons, light exercise and a place within the parish where they could gather and socialize.

Smaller class sizes in the parish school were also a blessing to both students and teachers, who had long struggled with crowded conditions involving fifty or more students squeezed into a single classroom with only one teacher. In order to serve the needs of all the students—both high achievers and those who required a bit more help in absorbing the material—aides were introduced into the classroom in the late 1970s. These trained professionals continue to assist the teachers by helping everyone in class keep up with the daily lesson plan, while providing additional challenges to those who might be moving ahead more rapidly than others in the class.

ST. CECILIA SCHOOL: FACTS AND FIGURES

- *In 1976, the first classroom aide, Teri DeBenedetti Watters, a St. Cecilia graduate from the class of 1967, was hired, establishing a new position in the school. She soon transitioned into the role of teacher and remains on the job more than forty years later. Mrs. Watters is the first teacher at St. Cecilia School to have an adult child, her son Chris Watters, as a fellow faculty member.*

- *By the 1980–81 school year, there were only two Sisters remaining who were assigned full-time classroom duties.*

- *Due to reduced class sizes in Grades 1 through 8, the school's kindergarten was able to reopen in the 1980–81 school year, after being closed more than twenty years earlier due to overcrowding in the school building.*

- *In the 1981–82 school year, there were 581 children enrolled (following the re-implementation of kindergarten), with an average class size of 32.*

Monsignor McKay also placed a greater emphasis on parishioner involvement in parish affairs. Early in his pastorate, he formed a parish council, the first finance council, the first school board and an expanded Men's Club. As time went on and there was a resurgence of younger families in the parish during 1980s, he established a Young Mothers' Group.

Presenting offertory gifts at a 1977 school Mass. *Parish Archives.*

Monsignor McKay also took note of the increasing number of deaths among those in the "Greatest Generation," a term that later became associated with journalist Tom Brokaw's 1998 book about those Americans who came of age during the Great Depression and the World War II years. There were many new widows and widowers among longtime parish members in the 1980s, and Monsignor McKay soon instituted a new group, the Arimatheans (named for Joseph of

Confirmation certificate, 1979. *Courtesy Marina Simonian.*

The original Knights of St. Cecilia group, with Monsignor McKay in front row, at right, 1980. The group became "co-ed" during the pastorate of Monsignor Harriman. *Parish Archives.*

Arimathea, who allowed the body of Our Lord to be placed into his own tomb following the crucifixion), as an outreach group to those who were recently bereaved. Slowly but surely, the parish was continuing to change and evolve, while still meeting the needs of its members, just as it had been doing since 1917.

By 1980, security considerations had forced the parish to lock the church immediately after the daily 9:00 a.m. Mass, and Monsignor McKay determined that this situation had to change. He formed a new group, the Knights of St. Cecilia, consisting of retired men who could each devote one hour per week to monitoring the safety of both worshippers and the church edifice itself during the hours that Mass was not being offered. Today, the group has become co-ed, still providing a valuable service to the parish by ensuring that the house of the Lord remains open throughout the day for prayer and quiet contemplation.

The declining number of Sisters in the 1980s certainly posed challenges to the operation of the parish school. Monsignor McKay noted one positive outcome from this change—namely, that there were unused rooms in the convent that could accommodate the needs of an expanding music program, as well as provide space to an increasing number of parish organizations. The conversion began slowly, with the

Miss Kays and her seventh-grade class in the 1980–81 school year. Class sizes were becoming considerably smaller than in earlier times. *Courtesy McKeon family.*

Above: Pastor Monsignor McKay and school principal Sister Marilyn Murphy at the graduation ceremony, June 4, 1989. *Courtesy Harrington family.*

Left: Sister M. Theresa Agnes, longtime music teacher at St. Cecilia School, at the time of her retirement. With her is pastor Monsignor James P. McKay, attending his own farewell reception, June 1990. *Parish Archives.*

The podium (sometimes called an ambon or ambo), hand-carved by Samuel Berger. Many longtime parishioners can still envision Monsignor Collins reading the Gospel, preaching and making the weekly announcements from this spot on those foggy Sunday mornings so long ago. *Courtesy Lynn Goldfinger-Abram.*

remaining Sisters still maintaining the privacy of their community on the top floor of the building. Over the next twenty years, the conversion gradually continued until the year 2000, when the old chapel in the convent was removed and the space added to a newly constructed Collins Center, when its original home in the lower church was converted into a large multipurpose facility.

The 1989 Loma Prieta earthquake left St. Cecilia Parish largely unscathed, as parishioners reached out to help others in the city who had suffered some significant losses in both their temporal and their spiritual homes.

ANNUAL PARISH PICNIC

Parish picnics have long been popular events enjoyed by thousands. According to the handwritten records of the first pastor, Father John Tobin, the very first parish picnic was held at Congress Springs Park in Saratoga in the fall of 1918, when he hired two buses to transport attendees. Although not held every single year since then, the event enjoyed renewed popularity in the 1960s, when parish membership hit an all-time high and the school's student body peaked at more than eight hundred students. Events were sometimes held at the old Marin Town & Country Club in Fairfax or at Morton's Warm Springs in Sonoma County, although Blackberry Farm in Cupertino has also been a popular locale for decades—surprisingly, the location is only five miles from the site of the 1918 picnic. Bringing together everyone from infants and toddlers to great-grandparents, the event continues to provide an opportunity for all members of the parish community to enjoy a day of food, fun and fellowship with one another. At one time, the 8:00 a.m. Sunday Mass at St. Cecilia Church was literally packed to overflowing on the morning of the picnic, but in recent times, the pastor has celebrated an outdoor Mass at the picnic site just prior to the commencement of festivities.

Chapter 6

A PERIOD OF TRANSITION

1990–1994

O n July 1, 1990, Archbishop John Quinn promoted St. Cecilia pastor Monsignor James McKay to the position of vicar general and moderator of the Curia for the Archdiocese of San Francisco. At the same time, he also appointed Monsignor Patrick O'Shea as the fifth pastor of St. Cecilia Parish.

Parishioners helped to complete the self-study required of all parishes in the archdiocese at that time. Each and every parish examined its programs to determine how they might better serve the needs of the local community.

Many parishes, like St. Cecilia, with an active school and numerous outreach programs designed to serve a diverse community, fared well in the self-study and were able to continue to minister to the various needs of parish members. In particular, it was noted that many of those who were the heads of young families during the school's highest enrollment years in the 1950s and 1960s (when it was often at or sometimes beyond its capacity of eight hundred students) were now retirees, advancing well into their senior years. Many were living alone, having lost a longtime spouse, and with their adult children living elsewhere. The parish began a greater outreach effort to these parishioners, and Father Heribert Duquet, in particular, took on a dedicated ministry to seniors, often delivering Holy Communion to well over one hundred housebound or nursing home residents each and every week of the year.

It was at this time that some other parishes in the city of San Francisco were determined to have ongoing needs that were not being thoroughly met,

Coaches Terry McHugh (left) and John Faulkner (right) pose with the eighth-grade boys' basketball team in 1992. *Courtesy Terry McHugh.*

and in some cases, a seriously declining parish membership that forced the archdiocese to make some difficult choices about whether or not certain communities remained economically viable. It was a difficult period for many longtime San Francisco Catholics.

Also, during the 1990s, disturbing reports were beginning to surface on a regular and fairly widespread basis about the prior and current personal conduct of some members of the Roman Catholic clergy throughout the United States and elsewhere. Sadly, members of the St. Cecilia Parish family were not spared from the awful impact of such crimes.

In retrospect, many different courses of action might have been taken, but at the time, few people recognized the true nature and scope of the problem. Also, the standard thinking of the era favored treatment in much the same way that addictions to alcohol and other substances might be addressed. Today, though, it has become clear that such approaches were ineffective and that those methods may have led to further harm for many. Now, with a new awareness, we all move forward, still trusting in the goodness of one another and praying for God's intercession to provide healing to the victims as we remain ever-vigilant to prevent future issues of this sort from ever happening again.

According to Victim Assistance Coordinator Dr. Renee Duffey of the Archdiocese of San Francisco, the official policy today is unmistakably clear: *"Anyone who has reason to believe, or might suspect, that a child has been abused, or is being abused, should report their suspicions first to civil authorities and then to the Archdiocese via its assigned Victim Assistance Coordinator."*

Traditional crucifix of the Sisters of the Holy Names of Jesus and Mary, awarded at the time of final vows and worn as part of the habit until the late 1960s. *Courtesy Sister Marilyn Miller, SNJM.*

"A Prayer for Healing Victims of Abuse"

God of endless love,
Ever caring, ever strong, always present, always just:
You gave your only Son over suffering and death.
Gentle Jesus, shepherd of peace,
Join to your own suffering
The pain of all who have been hurt
In body, mind, and spirit
By those who betrayed the trust placed in them.
Hear our cries as we agonize
Over the harm done to our brothers and sisters.
Breathe wisdom into our prayers,
Soothe restless hearts with hope,
Steady shaken spirits with faith:
Show us the way to justice and wholeness,
Enlightened by truth and enfolded in your mercy.
Holy Spirit, comforter of hearts,
Heal your people's wounds
And transform our brokenness.
Grant us courage and wisdom, humility and grace,
So that we may act with justice
And find peace in you. We ask this through Christ, our Lord. Amen.

(U.S. Conference of Catholic Bishops, 2004, reprinted with permission)

At the same time as the archdiocesan parish self-study was underway, there continued to be a strong focus on the maintenance and improvement of parish facilities. Additional unused rooms in the convent continued to be converted to space for various parish organizations.

St. Cecilia School: Facts and Figures

- *By the 1990–91 school year, there was only one Sister remaining who was assigned full time to the classroom, and she continued in this role until her retirement in June 2010.*
- *By the 1990s, different levels of tuition were beginning to be charged based on certain criteria: whether a family was active in the parish, contributing to the Sunday collection, performing service hours and if the student was a practicing Catholic.*

In 1992, St. Cecilia Parish celebrated its seventy-fifth anniversary in a more subdued fashion than during the Golden Jubilee year of 1967. The parish produced a book of remembrances that included professional portraits of several hundred parishioners and their families—an item that remains a keepsake in many households today.

PERSONAL REMINISCENCE: SISTER BERNICE BREEN (1920–2014)

Sister Bernice Breen (previously known as Sister Matthew of Mary) was a graduate of St. Cecilia School, class of 1944, who taught sixth grade for several years and then later returned, teaching fifth grade for nearly twenty more years. Sister had a love of poetry, and in 1992, she composed the following on the occasion of the parish's seventy-fifth anniversary. Although Sister went to be with the Lord in 2014, after sixty-two years of vowed religious life, her thoughts about St. Cecilia School still resound warmly with many people today:

"Ode to St. Cecilia School"

I salute you, St. Cecilia's, you've worn well,
Like a good coat, or a car that's swell.

You engender pride—and a bit of a smile—
Sparked by memories planted while
We were here in your walls, some of us long ago,
And in spite of the years, your worth does show.

When you were a single school, Grades 1 through 8,
Then the doors were locked if we were late;
Not many were late in those days of old;
Who, I ask, wanted to be out in the cold
When our friends were inside—good friends, too,
Whose warmth and friendship frequently pulled us through.

In studies, in plays, and even in team sports
We stuck together since space for courts
Was always small with classes good-size;
Having much space at all was quite a surprise!
And after-school sports were always fun
With room in the yard to skate and run
Then, as now, games were a delight
Every afternoon 'til early each night.
Why, it was on the old concrete wall
Where we first mastered the tennis ball!

Between the first bell and after school
We did work hard and followed the rule
Set down by the principal who ran a tight ship—
We were here every day, not one did we skip!

What has struck me for years and I say this to you
Is how much we learned, really mastered, too!
The Sisters were really fine teachers, I know,
Who really cared and worked so
That we would do well, as well as do good.
They taught skills and values, all that should
Equip us for life and the future to be—
I can't be grateful enough for what they gave to me.

I've returned twice as a teacher—in '70 and '81—
To join more fine teachers who continue the run
Of excellence in learning here in these walls
Through many springs and many falls.
What I loved is still here, I see it in faces
Hanging on walls and in other places
Like rallies, honors, parents, student families, science fair
Faculty meetings, candygrams, traffic patrol—always there!
It's a spirit, a bond, that reaches back in time.
It gives me a lift; it's easier to climb
Upward and outward—to do the good,
To see the beauty as much as I should.

It's there to be done and it's there to be seen;
My part's in the doing and I must be keen,
And so must you, for we're all part of a plan,
And, if we do what we're able, as much as we can,
The joy will be ours, and our school will grow,
It's been good to share with you—and so…

Although I'm not Frost, it has been fun
To muse on this spot under the sun—
My ALMA MATER, special and true,
Part of me and part of you!

Sister Bernice Breen,
 Class of 1944

In the fall of 1993, Archbishop John R. Quinn announced the closure of thirteen Catholic churches in San Francisco. St. Cecilia was not among those slated to be closed, and our parish was able to welcome new members from elsewhere in the archdiocese who were seeking a new spiritual home. The bonds of community grew tighter as traditional "parish boundaries" were relaxed and local Catholics were permitted to join any parish of their own choosing. St. Cecilia Parish began welcoming new members from throughout the city of San Francisco, as well as from northern San Mateo County.

A Period of Transition

Throughout the early 1990s, the parish plant was upgraded with improved night lighting for evening recreation in the schoolyard and a new plaza in front of the church.

Monsignor O'Shea resigned in the spring of 1994.

Do You Remember...?

Depending on the years a student attended St. Cecilia School, there were some long-remembered traditions and customs, including...

- *The white picket fence separating the "upper yard" where the church now stands from the "lower yard"?*
- *The mess in the schoolyard when the new church was under construction?*
- *The "Blessing of Throats" on St. Blaise Day, February 3 each year?*
- *How the cloak room in each classroom smelled something like a wet dog on rainy days?*
- *The red-and-blue cardboard sign at the front of the classroom reading, "To-morrow Is Bank Day" and, on the reverse, "To-day Is Bank Day"?*
- *When Religion was always the first subject each day?*
- *When art was always the final subject on Friday afternoons?*
- *How San Francisco generally had a heat wave during both the first week of school each September and during the last week of school each June?*
- *The cafeteria ladies?*
- *The smell of fish cakes from the cafeteria pervading the entire building on Fridays?*
- *Folding brown paper to make book covers?*
- *In the parish's very early days, the social events and picnics (complete with oom-pah-pah bands) sponsored by the athletic and social groups consisting of the many German and German American parishioners?*
- *When you went to your neighborhood drugstore at the start of each year for a free empty cigar box in which to store desk supplies?*
- *Having a piece of rolled up "oilcloth" in your desk to cover the top during art and craft projects?*
- *The covered walkway from the 18th Avenue entrance to the school so that the Sisters were protected from rain when walking back and forth to the convent?*
- *The piece of clear, firm plastic that the Sisters placed inside their white starched headpieces (known as coifs) so that they would not droop in foggy weather?*
- *When the only "appropriate" gifts for a nun were a pen, a box of stationery, handkerchiefs or homemade cookies?*

- *When your mother would give you a bunch of flowers from your backyard for Sister to place in a vase on the shelf in front of the statue of the Blessed Mother at the front of the classroom?*
- *The janitor arriving at your classroom with a bucket of sawdust to clean up "accidents"?*
- *Getting out early for "rainy day session"?*
- *Clapping erasers against each other in the schoolyard after school to clean them?*
- *Collecting canned goods for the Little Sisters of the Poor at Thanksgiving?*
- *The Toys for Tots drive at Christmastime?*
- *Advent wreaths with three purple candles and one pink candle?*
- *The smell of mimeograph fluid on all those papers handed out in class?*
- *When girls who forgot their uniform hats wore a small handkerchief or even a piece of Kleenex on their heads when entering the church and how Monsignor Collins hated to see these things and bandanas instead of a proper hat?*
- *The popularity of black lace mantillas in place of a hat for girls and women in the late 1960s?*
- *Practicing how to genuflect in front of the class in first grade?*
- *Lifting the hinged lid of your desk so that you could talk to your classroom neighbor?*
- *Dropping your pencil so that you could pass a note to your classroom neighbor?*
- *Wondering if the Sisters (before 1967) had their heads shaved underneath those veils?*
- *How no one ever saw a nun eating, drinking from a school water fountain or going to the girls' bathroom?*
- *But how Sister did supervise and impose quiet in the boys' bathroom, much to the embarrassment of the older boys?*
- *Collecting money for the "far-away" Missions?*
- *Collecting money for the Pope's Poor campaign during Lent?*
- *Giving up candy for Lent?*
- *When transistor radios first came out?*
- *When hula hoops were the rage?*
- *When yo-yos became a fad (several different times)?*
- *When everyone was playing bongo drums at after-school volleyball games?*
- *Squirting your friends in the schoolyard by placing one finger on the drinking fountain spigot?*
- *Graduating eighth graders bursting into every classroom in the school on their last day of class to say goodbye to their former teachers?*

- The "Prophecies" prepared by each graduating class about the likely future lives of classmates? (Some of those written in 1966 and recently reviewed for the fiftieth reunion of that class proved to be highly accurate in many cases.)
- Bringing in one favorite Christmas gift to show the class on the first day back to school in January?
- Making a sign of the cross and saying a "Hail Mary" anytime that the siren of a passing police car, fire engine or ambulance could be heard?
- When the principal (also known as "Sister Superior" or "Soupy") had a wooden spoon on top of her desk as a visual reminder of a form discipline that was then still open to her?
- The big thrill when a few students were allowed to bring a portable television set to class in January 1961 so that everyone could watch the inauguration of John F. Kennedy?
- That fateful Friday afternoon in November 1963 (ironically, the Feast Day of St. Cecilia) when the public address system suddenly crackled to life midmorning with a radio broadcast announcing President Kennedy's assassination in Dallas, Texas?
- "Getting to Know You Day" in the 1950s, when each classroom would design its own artwork name badge, and students would then try to learn the names of as many teachers and students from other classrooms as possible—with the theme song coming from the 1951 Rodgers and Hammerstein musical The King and I?
- The beginning of programs like Kindergarten Buddies and School Families?
- The first Thanksgiving Retreat?
- Shopping with your Kindergarten Buddy at the Christmas Boutique in the lower church?
- Weekly dance lessons with Mrs. Hunter in the auditorium?
- May Procession and Crowning (a tradition going back to the very first years of the school)?
- Selling Holy Childhood Christmas seals to family and friends?
- Attending Stations of the Cross and Benediction in the lower church when the 1957 earthquake struck?
- The St. Cecilia–Holy Name annual sports tournament early each year since 1948?
- The beginning of "Extended Care" and "Drive-Through Drop-Off and Pick-Up?"
- How happy everyone was when there was a change in school uniforms to something new—about once every ten years?

- *How boys all hated their salt-and-pepper corduroy pants?*
- *When shoes had to be polished—black for the boys and white for the girls?*
- *Looking in the mirror and realizing that you are having a "bad hair day" on the morning that school pictures were being taken?*
- *Having seagulls swoop down on you in the schoolyard to try to take your sandwich?*
- *Filling your assigned time slot at 40 Hours' devotion.*
- *The excitement of an evening at the Parish Festival?*
- *The Dedication Day of the school expansion, the new church or the Durocher Pavilion?*
- *How some priests (like Father Riordan) always gave an easy penance during confession ("say two Hail Marys") and had long lines of people waiting outside his confessional? Other priests, who were known to give harsher penances ("say three rosaries, make a novena, put an extra dollar into the collection plate this week and give up candy for a month") never had anyone waiting to go to confession with them.*
- *When the desks still had inkwells, then when cartridge pens were used and then when ballpoint pens were used?*
- *When everyone decided to use "peacock blue" ink in the 1960s?*
- *When the school building was just eight classrooms?*
- *When kindergarten had to be closed down in 1957, and then when it came back in 1981?*
- *When we first heard about national tragedies, such as assassinations and attempts, 9/11 and the space shuttle disaster?*
- *When the linoleum floors at St. Cecilia School were still brown and the hallways were painted pink on the top and blue on the bottom?*
- *Field trips to the San Francisco Symphony?*
- *Paper drives, rag drives and used clothing drives?*
- *Not wanting to have anything negative recorded in your "permanent record"?*
- *Watching the clock on Friday afternoons when the hands moved very, very slowly?*
- *When the biggest thrill of the week involved someone wheeling the school's filmstrip projector/movie projector/TV and VCR (depending on your era) into the classroom for a special presentation?*
- *Attending First Friday Mass throughout the school year?*
- *Participating in Stations of the Cross on the Fridays during Lent?*
- *The purple coverings over the statues in church during the last two weeks of Lent, so that we would focus only on Christ himself and his suffering on the cross?*

- *Reviewing the new Legion of Decency film ratings each month in order to learn which movies you could or could not see?*
- *Selling subscriptions to the archdiocesan newspaper, the* Monitor, *each fall?*
- *Setting up Nativity scenes in the classroom each December?*
- *The student-produced broadcast on the public address system—"Station CFM, Come Follow Me"—that encouraged religious vocations? Father Charles Phipps, SJ, professor at Santa Clara University; Sister Ann Gilchrist, learning specialist at St. Cecilia School; and dozens of other Bay Area priests and nuns once sat in these classrooms, contemplating career choices.*
- *When a new American flag was introduced in the summer of 1960 to reflect the addition of two more stars—one for Alaska and one for Hawaii— bringing the total to fifty?*
- *Having long discussions at lunch and recess about the choice of confirmation names?*
- *The introduction of computers in the classroom and then laptops and tablets?*
- *Cupcake sales to support the Missions?*
- *Sno-cone days at lunchtime in the schoolyard during spring?*
- *Sisters reminding those who studied guitar that their chosen instrument was not part of the school band?*
- *The thrill of staying up late to attend Midnight Mass at Christmas or Easter for the very first time?*
- *The excitement when Monsignor Collins announced a dispensation from the rule about Friday abstinence from meat on the day after Thanksgiving and on St. Patrick's Day?*
- *The one or two times per year when Sister allowed the class to "change desks" during the school year?*
- *Being old enough to join the school's Traffic Safety Patrol?*
- *Going to the annual Traffic Safety Patrol Review held at the Polo Field or Kezar Stadium?*
- *The annual eighth-grade field trip to the state capitol and stopping off at the Milk Farm on the way home?*
- *The "musical staff chalkboard liners" that drew five parallel horizontal lines on the blackboard so that Sister could show musical notes properly?*
- *The small round chrome "pitch pipe" that Sister would use to get the entire class singing in the correct key?*
- *Standing at the blackboard in front of the entire class, chalk in hand, trying to diagram a sentence in the correct format of straight horizontal*

lines, with short vertical lines dividing subject, verb and object and with angled lines beneath each section for adjectives and adverbs?

- The first time you were brave enough to try a new, unknown food item at the Multicultural Day luncheon?
- Feeling proud when you were selected to raise and lower the flag on the Vicente Street flagpole?
- Classmates fainting in church because of the old rules on pre-Communion fasting?
- The excitement you felt the first time that you and your classmates performed for an audience on stage in the school auditorium?
- Your reaction to hearing your own voice booming out in the church the first time you were selected to do a reading?
- Standing and kneeling in church, in response to the sound of Sister's clapper?
- Taking "The Pledge" at the time of confirmation that you would abstain from alcohol until the age of twenty-one (no longer in use)?
- Studying to be an altar server—especially in those years when you had to learn Latin responses to the prayers?
- When Holy Communion was distributed to Mass attendees kneeling at the Communion rail, and altar server used to whack the paten against the throats of their friends?
- Being old enough and good enough to serve on the altar at weddings and funerals?
- When video streaming was first introduced at Mass in 2001?
- Learning prayers and Mass responses in first grade?
- Memorizing Catechism questions/answers in second grade?
- Learning about fractions and decimals in third grade?
- Singing American folk songs in fourth grade?
- Studying the California Missions in fifth grade?
- Learning about world history for the first time in sixth grade?
- Beginning to think about high school choices in seventh grade?
- Thinking that once eighth grade was over, things would be so much easier in high school?
- Reminders from teachers to eighth graders just before graduation: "You are on the top now, here in grammar school, but you will soon be on the bottom again, once you start high school"?
- Sitting at eighth-grade graduation and hearing the priest say, "This is the very last time that every single one of you will be in the same place at the same time, so take a good look around, because after today, you will never be together again in the way that you have been for the last eight years"? And he was right.

Longtime second-grade teacher Mrs. Catherine Ring, also the First Communion coordinator for many years, leads the singing at a 1990s liturgy. *Ring family photo.*

PERSONAL REMINISCENCE: VIRGINIA CONROY (1918–1993)

My husband and I were born and raised in the Mission District and started our family there after our wedding in 1940. Just before Ray's retirement from the San Francisco Fire Department, we moved to the Parkside District in 1973 with our two youngest children and became members of St. Cecilia Parish. We soon found ourselves among the warmest and friendliest neighbors imaginable and were quickly drawn into an active life in our new parish.

St. Cecilia School students, 2015–16 school year. *Parish Archives.*

Chapter 7

THE MONSIGNOR HARRIMAN ERA

1994–Present

On July 1, 1994, Archbishop Quinn announced the appointment of Father Michael Harriman as the sixth pastor of St. Cecilia Parish. Coming in at the completion of the parish's self-study, Father Harriman immediately set out to help implement the new Archdiocesan Pastoral Plan. Like most of his predecessors, Father Harriman was a skilled listener and sought input from parishioners on a number of major issues.

Within the first twelve months, he implemented several changes, such as the inclusion of girls in the altar server program, a change that had been authorized within the Catholic Church a number of years earlier. Today, more than twenty years later, it is routine to see girls serving alongside boys at Mass and other liturgical events at St. Cecilia Church, even though some other local Catholic parishes have been slower to embrace this longstanding liturgical change. In some cases, sister/brother siblings have served together on the altar in recent years.

Father Harriman also implemented a Chinese Ministry, with a goal of fostering friendship among the Chinese residents in the parish and to serve their needs in various ways, including Chinese RCIA classes, Bible sharing group, prayer meetings and classes for the study of the Chinese language and its dialects for schoolchildren.

As part of the listening sessions in the spring and fall of 1996, when the Archdiocesan Pastoral Plan was being implemented, many parishioners continued to express the need for a new multipurpose facility as part of the parish's physical plant. In late 1996, a committee was formed to study the

Monsignor Harriman, pastor for more than twenty years, officiating at a wedding in Our Lady's Chapel, 2014. *Courtesy Craig Wolfrom Photography.*

feasibility of such a construction effort, particularly the funding aspect. By the fall of 1997, parishioners were invited to participate in the "Giving for Our Future" campaign. Although some financial "experts" were of the opinion that the necessary $1.6 million could not be raised because of a reduced number of parish households over the prior twenty years, those in charge of fundraising were as confident in their ability to raise money as Monsignor Collins had been more than forty years earlier. In spite of some skeptics, members of the St. Cecilia Parish family—led by a dedicated fundraising committee co-chaired by Rosie Dominguez, Sally Mullkerrins and Tony Ribera—managed to exceed that goal, bringing in $1.8 million for construction of the new facility, thanks to the work of all those on the committee and the generous financial support from thousands of individual donors.

By the spring of 1998, architects were working on the design of the new building, with a clear mandate that such a structure be multipurpose and able to house formation programs and social events, as well as athletic activities. In addition, the architects also planned for the relocation of the Collins Center from the lower church to a new space adjacent to the old chapel of the St. Cecilia Convent. Times had changed, and there was no longer the need for a residential building housing twenty or more Sisters,

Pastor Michael Harriman, school principal Sister Marilyn Miller and Archbishop William Levada break ground for the Durocher Pavilion in May 1999. *Parish Archives.*

nor any need for a covered walkway to a private walled garden. While these were important considerations in earlier times, the needs of the parish community were quite different by the late 1990s, and members responded with traditional St. Cecilia Parish enthusiasm.

Construction of the new facility began in May 1999, and as it was nearing completion in December of that year, it was formally named the Durocher Pavilion, in honor of Blessed Marie-Rose Durocher, foundress of the Sisters of the Holy Names of Jesus and Mary, the religious order associated with St. Cecilia School since its opening in 1930. She had been beatified by Pope John Paul II (now a saint himself) in 1982—the final step in her path to canonization as a saint of the Roman Catholic Church.

The Durocher Pavilion was dedicated in May 2000 in a ceremony involving parishioners, students, parents, neighbors and many longtime former teachers and principals. In that same month, in the Jubilee Year of Our Lord, 2000, St. Cecilia pastor Reverend Michael D. Harriman was elevated to the position of monsignor. Within the Roman Catholic clergy, the title is bestowed on a priest who has distinguished himself by his service. The title is honorary rather than a specific position in religious hierarchy, so the duties of a monsignor remain the same as those of any other priest in a similar assignment. However, it is clearly seen as a fitting accolade for an individual who was able to accomplish so much in turning around a deeply troubled parish since being appointed to his assignment in 1994.

Under the leadership of Monsignor Harriman, the parish school has also continued to thrive. Technology, first introduced in the early 1990s by Sister Helen Walsh, was expanded to include computer use in many phases of the learning process. St. Cecilia School hired a long-serving lay teacher, Mr. Gene Ide, as the first technology coordinator. Today, under his leadership, laptop computers and tablets are present in all classrooms to assist students in achieving their academic goals.

Careful financial management of the funds entrusted to the Monsignor Harold Collins School Fund (which was established under Monsignor McKay's leadership immediately after the passing of Monsignor Collins in December 1980) resulted in the balance of the fund reaching $1 million within the first decade after its establishment in 1980 and to $2 million by the turn of the millennium. Today, the account continues to grow and has surpassed $3 million, with income used to defray the cost of tuition for students in St. Cecilia School.

The school has also benefitted from Monsignor Harriman's support of many new programs:

BOARD OF COMMISSIONERS: This group was established to function in the same manner as a high school student council, with class representatives from the upper grades and others elected to discuss and provide input on many school-related matters.

KINDERGARTEN BUDDIES: This program was developed early in the new millennium, assigning each kindergarten student a same-gender "Big Buddy" who can answer questions, be a recognizable face on the schoolyard, help with homework and prevent bullying before it ever has a chance to start.

For the older students, it provides experience in assuming responsibility, planning for unforeseen events and offering a voice of reason to younger schoolmates. Students, teachers and parents have all given the program an enthusiastic thumbs-up.

Multicultural Day: This annual fall event, celebrating culture through cuisine, is an all-day activity in the school auditorium. With the strong support of the Mothers' Club, hot and cold food items—including appetizers, entrées and desserts—are prepared and served, as groups of students display dance and musical performances, often in native costumes, from every region of the world.

School Families: In an era when many children have far fewer siblings than in the past (or often none at all), this organization brings together one child from each grade level into a group that will progress through their school years together. These groups meet monthly and have resulted in friendships that have endured well beyond the years of elementary school.

Service Hours: Each student's volunteer time and participation in various programs that benefit the parish and the local community are formally accounted for. This is similar to what has been in place for many years at most local Catholic high schools.

Monsignor Harriman also instituted other significant activities, such as the Post-Thanksgiving Retreat, a popular parish event for more than fifteen years. It offers participants a unique opportunity to step away from the hectic pace of life on a busy weekend—at a time when giving thanks sometimes vies head-on with commercialism. Many parishioners regard the event as an important part of their spiritual approach to the Christmas season.

The parish's ongoing support for the school has ensured that no significant outlays are needed for advertising—parents themselves actively seek out St. Cecilia School for their children. Monsignor has also engaged in various outreach programs to recruit new parishioners so that the parish might continue to have a broad base of members serving as active participants in a faith-based community.

Now, as he leads us in the centennial celebration of St. Cecilia Parish, he is known within the community—simply and most affectionately—as "Our Pastor."

PERSONAL REMINISCENCE: MONSIGNOR MICHAEL HARRIMAN

Shortly after I was appointed pastor more than twenty years ago, the decision was made to expand the use of computers within our school. Even with teacher Mr. Gene Ide and the fathers of the parish donating free labor for construction, studies indicated that just over $60,000 in cash would be needed for converting a storage space into a computer lab—a significant expenditure for us at that time. Much as we wanted to move forward, we had just a small fraction of that amount available, thus putting the whole project far out of our reach. You can imagine my surprise when a check from a San Francisco law firm, for a significant sum and made payable to St. Cecilia Parish, soon arrived in the afternoon mail—an extremely generous bequest from the estate of longtime parishioner Jacqueline Tinney, who was a graduate of our parish school more than fifty years earlier—a gift for which we had no advance notice whatsoever. When I spoke with the family to express my gratitude, they whole-heartedly agreed with the idea of using the money to benefit the school, and when I walked over to share the good news with Principal Sister Marilyn Miller, she literally had tears in her eyes, remarking on this clear miracle of divine intervention. Today, a framed photo of Miss Tinney graces the wall of the computer facility that was named in her honor. May we always be blessed with such generosity from members of our parish family!

CURRENT PARISH ORGANIZATIONS AND MINISTRIES

St. Cecilia Parish is made up of nearly two thousand households, encompassing families with children, empty-nesters, singles and the widowed/divorced/separated. Parishioners are of all ages, backgrounds and income levels. Some are lifelong members of the St. Cecilia family, and some are relative newcomers. The current parish organizations and ministries offer both spiritual and temporal support to all, and the parish welcomes participation in the outreach efforts to others.

Altar Servers

Boys and girls who are in the fifth grade through the eighth grade in our parish school or in a public school have an opportunity to serve the parish at the celebration of the Eucharistic liturgy on weekdays and Sundays. Candidates participate in a preparation program. Girls have been included in this program since Monsignor Harriman became pastor in 1994. Early in the new millennium, the program was expanded to include "streamers"—students who operate the video equipment that enables broadcasts of Sunday Mass, funerals, weddings and other events to at-home viewers.

Annual Festival

The principal social event of our parish year and an important fundraiser for the parish school, the annual festival is held in the month of October and has been an ongoing event since 1948. Under the guidance of the Festival Committee, a large number of our parishioners work together to produce a three-day time of celebration and sociability, while generating funds for our school. The festival now includes both indoor and outdoor activities, as it spreads out from the school auditorium, across the schoolyard and into the Durocher Pavilion. The event also provides an opportunity for parishioners to get to know one another a bit better.

Athletic Department

This program, in place since the 1950s, offers opportunities for the young people of our parish to participate in a number of organized sports. The goal of the sports program is to offer one more opportunity for growth as a person and in relationships with others during her/his elementary school years. St. Cecilia is a participant in the Positive Coaching Alliance.

Baptismal Catechesis

When a family wishes to have their child baptized, they, and the godparents, participate in a special preparation program. This program is offered the third Tuesday every month from 7:30 p.m. to 9:00 p.m. in the Collins Center, 2560 18th Avenue. As soon as a baptism is anticipated, parents should contact the rectory.

Children's Faith Formation (CFF)

Children's Faith Formation is offered for Catholic students attending public schools and for preschool and kindergarten ages. Classes are held on Sunday mornings from 9:00 a.m. to 10:30 a.m., and this includes the 9:30 a.m. Mass. It takes place in the Collins Center and in the former convent. All parishioners who have children in public schools are urged to register them in the CFF program.

Chinese Ministry

The Chinese Ministry goal is to foster friendship among the Chinese members of our parish and to serve their needs in various ways. The programs available are Chinese RCIA classes, Bible sharing group, prayer meetings and Chinese language classes for schoolchildren. The group was founded during the pastorate of Monsignor Harriman.

Children attending Chinese New Year celebration, lower church, 2010. *Courtesy Rio Kim.*

Collins Center

The Monsignor Harold E. Collins Center is located at 2560 18ᵗʰ Avenue next to the former convent. The center is the hub of a number of social, educational and recreational activities, many of which are focused on the needs of seniors. The first director of the Collins Center was Sister Jeanne Cusick, who served the needs of the parish's growing senior community—particularly coordinating travel adventures. Other regular activities at the Collins Center include language lessons, hobbies such as knitting and crochet, films, book discussions and alumni events. Diane Weinkauf is the current coordinator. All are welcome to drop in to read the many magazines and periodicals, attend a class, register for an outing or simply to visit with other parishioners over a cup of coffee.

Confirmation Preparation Team

A parish priest, our youth minister and high school youth conduct a nine-month program preparing our young people for the sacrament of confirmation. Those wishing to receive this sacrament should submit a formal request in the fall of each year in order to be enrolled in the program. Candidates must be in the seventh grade or older.

Eucharistic Ministers

This group brings together parishioners who are commissioned to distribute the Eucharist. They bring Holy Communion to those who are confined at home or in convalescent facilities. They also assist with the distribution of the Eucharist during Mass.

Filipino Community

This is a group of Filipino parishioners who meet to support their culture, while helping them to integrate into the parish family. They celebrate some traditional devotions, and they also gather weekly for "Block Rosary" meetings. This group also sponsors the annual Santo Nino Novena, which is held in December, and the May Festival every spring. The group was formed in December 1979, early in the pastorate of Monsignor McKay.

Finance Committee

The Finance Committee, established by Monsignor McKay in the early 1980s, is a group of parishioners that meets monthly to review and evaluate the financial status of the parish. This group prepares the annual report to the parish and advises the pastor in the area of finance.

First Steps in Faith

This CFF (Children's Faith Formation) program is for children who are four and five years of age. Classes are held in the lower church during the 9:30 a.m. Mass each Sunday during the school year.

High School Youth Group

Under the direction of our youth minister, the youth group meets once a month on Sundays from 6:00 p.m. to 7:30 p.m. The purpose of these Sunday sharing sessions is to bring our faith alive. This group also offers recreational opportunities and service projects for its members. All high school–age parishioners are invited to join our St. Cecilia Youth Group. Please look at the "button" on the main page of the parish website.

Indonesian Community

This parish organization is involved in traditional Indonesian culture and devotional activities among parish members. The group also supports the work of a small community of Indonesian Carmelite nuns living on the top floor of the old parish convent.

Italian Catholic Federation (ICF)

Branch No. 365 of this large statewide organization meets in St. Cecilia Parish. It is composed of members from a number of parishes in our neighborhood. ICF sponsors a number of social events throughout the calendar year and also supports religious and charitable causes.

Knights of St. Cecilia

First established by Monsignor McKay in 1980, this is a group of retired men and women who are committed to the care of our church. Each "Knight" is present for one hour in the church from 10:00 a.m. until 5:00 p.m. once a week, Monday through Saturday. Because of their presence, the church is always open to those who wish to visit and pray. Knights also provide for many other needs around our church and parish, and the group meets monthly.

League of the Sacred Heart

This is a women's group whose primary purpose is to provide the supplies for parish liturgical services and to care for the altar and its appointments. In addition, the ladies of the league provide a number of programs for the mutual support of their members and annually sponsor a number of social events. Group members frequently participate in funeral liturgies held at St. Cecilia Church. The league is the oldest parish organization still in existence, tracing its founding all the way back to the establishment of the parish in 1917. Along with the parish itself, members of the league will also be celebrating the group's centennial in 2017.

Officers for ICA Branch no. 365—St. Cecilia Parish. *Basuino photo.*

The first St. Cecilia cookbook was published in 1969 by members of the League of the Sacred Heart as a fundraiser for the parish school. *Courtesy Jo Anne Quinn.*

Lectors

This is a group of men and women of our parish family who exercise a vital role in the church's liturgical services. Lectors read the scriptures, offer the Prayers of the Faithful and lead the assembly in worship.

Legion of Mary

This organization places strong emphasis on the spiritual development of its members, especially through special devotion to Mary. Members also engage in a variety of outreach programs geared to assisting and supporting those in need.

Liturgy Committee

This group has the responsibility for reviewing and evaluating all aspects of the liturgical life of our parish. The committee also plans and implements the music, church decorations, seasonal celebrations and other elements of the liturgy.

Maintenance Committee

This group includes parishioners who are experienced in various trades and who are able to share their knowledge of construction, painting, electrical work and so on by advising and overseeing the constant maintenance which is required for the buildings and grounds of St. Cecilia Parish.

Marriage Preparation

When a man and a woman become engaged, they begin their preparation for the sacrament of matrimony. All couples planning to receive the sacrament must allow six months for a period of preparation. In order to assist the couples in their preparation, the archdiocese provides a series of sessions designed to offer matters for reflection and sharing. It is hoped that the sharing of experiences by committed married couples will be a source of information and encouragement for those contemplating marriage.

Each year, the Men of St. Cecilia group hosts a "Pancake Breakfast with Santa" that is very popular among families with school-age children. Pictured is a third-generation St. Cecilia family during Advent 2014. *Mike Huynh photo.*

Men of St. Cecilia (MOSC)

This organization is for the men of the parish. The goal is to bring the men together socially so that they might serve all members of our St. Cecilia Parish family. The annual Golf Day, Advent Pancake Breakfast and Work Days completing school repairs and maintenance are examples of their dedicated service to the parish.

Mothers' Club

This organization is made up of mothers whose children attend St. Cecilia School or the parish CCD program. The mothers are given the opportunity to develop friendships and provide mutual support through the spiritual, educational and social activities that are offered. The Mothers' Club also organizes volunteer assistance for our parish school and sponsors fundraising events. Meetings of the general membership are held monthly.

Music/Choir

Music is an essential part of worship and liturgical prayer. Singers and musicians, principally members of our parish, volunteer to share their talents in the preparation and presentation of the music that enhances our liturgical services. Musical leaders are employed to help us worship and praise God through song. Music directors plan singing for the assembly, and cantors lead the community in songs and responses. A group of dedicated parishioners form the parish choir, which enhances the liturgy at the 11:30 a.m. Mass on Sunday and on the major feasts throughout the year. There is also a children's choir that sings monthly.

Post-Thanksgiving Retreat

The first Post-Thanksgiving Retreat was held in November 2000 on the Friday, Saturday and Sunday after Thanksgiving at CYO Camp in Occidental. It brought together children, high school youth, senior parishioners and married couples, and there were about fifty participants every year for some fifteen years. With the help of parishioners John and Mary Lee, Sally Mulkerrins and Charley Lavery, the program provided a unique opportunity to step away from the hectic pace of life for a few days of spiritual nourishment.

Rite of Christian Initiation for Adults (RCIA)

RCIA is a journey in faith. It is a process of conversion and learning more about the Catholic Church. It is meant especially for adults who are interested in becoming Catholic or just learning about the Catholic Church. It can bring us closer to our God and brother, Jesus Christ, and our Roman Catholic faith community.

Sacristans

This is a group made up of parishioners who prepare the altar for every Mass. They also oversee and care for all of the vestments, vessels and equipment that are used in our church. Finally, they are present to assist the priests in their preparations for liturgical services and devotions.

School of Pastoral Leadership

Sponsored by the Archdiocese of San Francisco, this is a one-year formation program to enable the laity to serve the parish in various areas of ministry. The school meets once a week for two semesters and provides both general instruction on the church and specific training in an elective area of your choice. Interested persons may contact the rectory for more information.

St. Cecilia Parish School

One of the important responsibilities of our parish is the education and religious formation of our children. Under the leadership of the Sisters of the Holy Names of Jesus and Mary, the school provides a Catholic education for approximately six hundred students from kindergarten to the eighth grade, thanks to the dedicated work of fifty-three lay women and men. In this new millennium, it is the largest K–8 Catholic school in the Archdiocese of San Francisco.

The student body of St. Cecilia School in the schoolyard adjacent to the lower church, 2010–11 school year. Today, St. Cecilia is the largest K–8 Catholic school in the San Francisco Archdiocese. *Parish Archives.*

St. Vincent de Paul Society

This spiritually oriented society provides assistance for parish families who find themselves in need of financial support or assistance. The society depends on the generous contributions of goods and money from our parish family to carry out its important Christian mission.

Ushers

Ushers are available at all major Masses and services to greet parishioners and guests, assist with the seating, take up the collection and respond to any needs that may arise.

Youth Ministry

Our youth ministry helps young people keep in touch with former classmates who are in different high schools and also serves as a place for them to bring new friends. Activities such as Daily Spiritual Reflections online, Ice Breakers and Open Gym are all available. Any high school student in the in the parish and their friends from other parishes are welcome. There is a Sunday monthly meeting on a specific theme, and the group's goal is to deal with timely issues in the light of our faith. Once a month, the Youth Group is in charge of the 9:30 a.m. Family Mass, where members may participate as greeters, lectors and gift bearers, as well as preparing donuts and coffee for fellow parishioners after Mass. Members may also have leadership roles in the annual Post-Thanksgiving Retreat, sophomores may apply to be on the confirmation team and seniors may apply to be on the team for the eighth-grade retreat.

IMAGES OF THE PARISH IN THE NEW MILLENNIUM

Top: Co-chairs of the original committee Rosie Dominguez, Sally Mulkerrins and Tony Ribera lead guests to the dedication ceremony for the Durocher Pavilion, May 2000. *Parish Archives.*

Middle: Dedication ceremony for the Durocher Pavilion, May 2000. The completion of this long-awaited goal marked a new beginning for the parish in the new millennium. *Parish Archives.*

Bottom: Four principals (past and current) of St. Cecilia School at the dedication of the Durocher Pavilion in May 2000. *Left to right*: Sister Michaeline Falvey (Sister Michaeline Mary), principal from 1957 to 1962 and prior teacher; Sister Marilyn Miller (Sister M. Ann Kristin), principal from 1992 to 2012; Sister Sylvia Bartheld (Sister M. Catherine Elizabeth), principal from 1968 to 1974 and prior teacher; and Sister Marilyn Murphy (Sister Andrew Marie), principal from 1979 to 1992 and prior teacher. *Parish Archives.*

PERSONAL REMINISCENCE: MS. VERONICA GRANUCCI

Our family has a long history at St. Cecilia School, including my grandfather Ron Granucci (class of 1954), plus my mother, Claudia Uribe Granucci (1981), and all of her sisters: Lily Uribe Angelopoulos (1985), Nelly Uribe Fabre (1988) and Sandy Uribe Gonzales (1992). I graduated in 2004, my cousin Sofia Angelopoulos [in] 2014 and my brother Estefan Granucci [in] 2015. All the rest of my cousins on my mother's side are current students.

I am a member of the St. Cecilia class of 2004 and am one of the fairly recent graduates on staff—not the youngest, but one of them! Since graduating I initially stayed connected to the school through my brother Estefan. My aunt Lily Uribe Angelopoulos was the alumni director before me and eventually drafted me onto the alumni board a few years ago. I loved helping her keep the alumni community connected, so when she stepped down, I was lucky to have the opportunity to move into her role.

Some of my favorite memories as a St. Cecilia student were from the festival, student families and sports. It's fun to share those memories with my brother and cousins, who are former and current students as well, because they have been able to experience the very same things and then some.

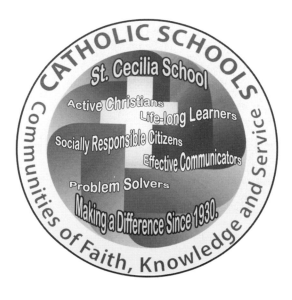

Poster from Catholic Schools Week, 2013–14 school year. *Parish Archives.*

ST. CECILIA SCHOOL: FACTS AND FIGURES

- *By the end of the 2009–10 school year, Sister Margaret Kinzie (the last remaining Holy Names Sister who was assigned to regular classroom duties) retired, and lay teachers then became 100 percent of the school's regular teaching staff, leaving a single Holy Names nun, Sister Marilyn Miller, as principal. Sister Margaret then took on the role of music director, with Sister Ann Gilchrist as a learning specialist—positions still held by each of them today.*

- *Today, the convent building contains an office for the director of the Collins Center, two offices for the school's learning specialists, the PE director's office and a meeting room for Collins Center activities. The second floor contains six piano rooms that are also used on Sundays for Children's Faith Formation classes, and the third floor is home to a small group of Charismatic Carmelite nuns from Indonesia that have been a community here for the last three years.*

- *At the end of the 2011–12 school year, Sister Marilyn Miller, the last Holy Names principal, retired. The very first lay principal, Mrs. Marian Connelly, a St. Cecilia School graduate and a member of the faculty for nearly thirty years, was then appointed to lead the school.*

- *Beginning with the 2012–13 school year, assistant principal became a full-time position, just as it has been in the public school system.*

Back-to-school rally, Durocher Pavilion, September 2012. *Parish Archives.*

Opening Mass, 2011–12 school year, showing eighth graders paired with their "Kindergarten Buddies." *Parish Archives.*

First day of school, 2011–12 school year, with students organizing supplies during the afterschool Extended Care program in the former cafeteria location. Today, this space is used for two new kindergarten classrooms, with Extended Care relocated to the auditorium. *Parish Archives.*

Group of eighth graders and their Kindergarten Buddies at Larsen Park, 2012. Today, these eighth graders have moved on to college, as the onetime kindergarteners are now approaching their middle school years. *Parish Archives.*

In the St. Cecilia classrooms of today (shown here in the 2010–11 school year), learning is a far more collaborative experience than in the past. Desks can still be arranged into individual rows when standardized testing takes place. *Parish Archives.*

Christmas art project, 2012–13 school year. *Parish Archives.*

Students entering church, 2009–10 school year. *Parish Archives.*

Opposite, top: Classroom aides offer personalized attention to students, shown here in the 2010–11 school year, while supporting the lesson plans implemented by the teachers. The first aide was hired for St. Cecilia School in the mid-1970s, and she soon transitioned to the role of teacher; forty years later, she is continuing to serve the needs of the parish school and its students. *Parish Archives.*

Opposite, bottom: Technology was introduced to St. Cecilia School by Sister Helen Walsh and Mr. Gene Ide beginning in 1990 with the first computer skills classes. Today, technology is incorporated into all phases of classroom activities, and students have wireless computer access in every classroom, as shown here (on a uniform-less Free Dress Day) in the 2010–11 school year. *Parish Archives.*

Above: Monsignor Mickey McCormick (left), assigned to St. Cecilia Parish for five years, joins pastor Monsignor Harriman and altar servers in the vestibule of the church for May Procession, 2011. *Parish Archives.*

Left: May Procession participants, 2011. The annual event in honor of the Blessed Mother is one of the longest continuously held religious services in the school's history, going back nearly ninety years. *Parish Archives.*

ST. CECILIA PARISH IN THE NEWS

At a time when employers are seeking highly qualified candidates in a very competitive work environment, the Men of St. Cecilia (MOSC) group began working with the alumni coordinator in 2014 to assist recent graduates of St. Cecilia School, as noted in the following news article:

- JOB FAIR—Saturday Dec. 19, 2015, 1:00 pm—4:00 pm, Durocher Pavilion—The Men of St. Cecilia in conjunction with the St. Cecilia Alumni Association are excited to announce our second annual job fair for alumni of St. Cecilia School. The goal of this venture is to bring together Bay Area business representatives to meet with St. Cecilia graduates from the years 2006–2015 (currently in high school and college) to discuss their companies and potentially provide summer internship and job opportunities to qualified candidates. The graduates will be able to have face-to-face interaction with these representatives to help broaden their knowledge of what the job market has to offer and to get ideas on how to reach their goals.

Art teacher Ann Basuino (right) with student Virginia Fabi (left) and her painting of Christ the King during art show in the lower church in 2010. Ms. Basuino has also been responsible for the painstaking hand restorations of several of the statues in St. Cecilia Church. *Parish Archives.*

Girls' sports team on Spirit Day, Durocher Pavilion, St. Cecilia–Holy Name Parish Tournament, 2012. *Parish Archives.*

Boys' seventh-grade soccer team, 2015. *Parish Archives.*

The St. Cecilia Drama Club Presents
The Janessa Greig Spring Musical
10th Anniversary Production of

THE
GHOSTLIGHT:
A MUSICAL REVUE

May 3 & 4, 7pm || May 5, 2pm
Mercy High School Theater
3250 19th Avenue, San Francisco
Tickets Go On Sale Mid April

Program for the 2013 school play, designed by a St. Cecilia parent. *Courtesy Monica Loos.*

Students performing Irish dance for the student body, 2011–12 school year. *Parish Archives.*

Father Elias Salomon, a parochial vicar who served at St. Cecilia Church, along with students in the school auditorium on Multicultural Day, 2008. *Parish Archives.*

Multicultural Day festivities include sampling cuisines from around the globe. *Parish Archives.*

Opposite, bottom: Faculty members Sue Wilson Holland (class of 1973) and Darin Fong (class of 1986) attending annual Alumni Sunday Mass, January 2012. *Parish Archives.*

Girls' dance group performing at the Durocher Pavilion, Multicultural Day 2013. *Parish Archives.*

PERSONAL REMINISCENCE: MR. DARIN FONG

As a present-day faculty member, one of my greatest memories from my student days is just walking to and from school in the 1980s. Back in those days, many more kids walked to school versus being driven; drive-through didn't even exist. Instead, we had student crossing guards on all the street corners before and after school. After hanging around in the school yard, we would walk home, and some of our strongest friendships were built on those walks. Kids were allowed to be kids, and they discussed all the important matters of the day: what happened on a certain TV show, new music from a particular band, if the Niners were going to go to the Superbowl, how our own teams were doing in whatever sport was going on and so forth. Walking home also allowed us to explore our neighborhood and learn the ways of the world. For example, we would walk into Pinelake Market to buy a soda or a candy bar after baseball practice. Afterwards, we would carry on our deep discussions over in the schoolyard of Parkside School on 25th Avenue and Vicente (which is now Dianne Feinstein School) or just continue walking on our journey home before it got dark. This would start in the fourth grade for most of us. We were fortunate enough to have a lot more independence than most of the kids today.

Theresa Schoenstein and Anne Bosque Collins, graduates of St. Cecilia School (class of 1937), reminiscing seventy-five years later on the first floor of the school building, Alumni Sunday, January 2012. *Parish Archives.*

PERSONAL REMINISCENCE: NANCY MAZZA

I grew up on 15th Avenue near Vicente as the oldest of three children in an Irish-Italian family. I graduated from St. Cecilia School in 1962, and my two brothers followed me in 1964 and 1969. I have been involved in selling real estate in San Francisco for more than thirty years now, and even I am constantly amazed by the prices. There is a definite desire on the part of many young families to live in the neighborhood around St. Cecilia School and to send their children there. Whenever I manage to bring together a buyer and a seller after sometimes difficult negotiations, I am always so pleased to see everyone's reactions. My face lights up as much as the faces of the new owners to think that another family will experience the same sort of close-knit community that our family did and that the children will get a great educational foundation that will support them well into the twenty-second century!

First Eucharist group, 2012. *Parish Archives.*

St. Cecilia School Annual Fundraiser
Saturday, March 29, 2014
Durocher Pavilion

Program from a 2014 school fundraiser. The record-breaking event netted $135,000 for the school. *Parish Archives.*

PERSONAL REMINISCENCE: ANDRELIZ BAUTISTA MCGLADE

I grew up in San Francisco and attended Notre Dame des Victoires before graduating from St. Rose Academy in the 1980s. While I was in high school, I was always impressed with the educational backgrounds of my many friends who had gone to St. Cecilia School. So, when my husband and I were trying to decide on a kindergarten for our older daughter, we knew that we wanted a Catholic school but something close to home. We were leaning toward a school in a nearby parish, but then we attended the open house at St. Cecilia. After meeting the teachers, we were so impressed with the sense of community here, involving parents, siblings and entire families, as well as the school's diversity. As we met many of the long-term teachers like Mrs. Watters, Miss Kays and others, it became an easy choice. Our older daughter loves her classmates and teachers, and she looks forward to each new day, while her younger sister is so excited about starting here in just a few more years. Meanwhile, I've reconnected with a lot of my St. Rose friends in the Mothers' Club, while my husband, who grew up on the East Coast, is enjoying all the new families that he's meeting because of his coaching activities and taking prospective parents on tours of the school.

Young shoppers attend the Christmas Boutique, held each year in the lower church. Volunteers provide complimentary wrapping, and younger shoppers are helped by their older eighth-grade "Buddies" to make gift selections for their family members. *Parish Archives.*

Field trips have long provided students with additional levels of enrichment that cannot be covered in the classroom. This third-grade class enjoyed a performance of the San Francisco Symphony at the Louise M. Davies Symphony Hall in December 2015. The author and his seventh-grade St. Cecilia School classmates enjoyed a similar field trip to a symphony performance at the Civic Auditorium exactly fifty years earlier. *Courtesy Mary Ellen (MER) Ring.*

Video cameras positioned in the choir loft allow the broadcast of Mass on Sundays and holy days, plus other events such as weddings and funerals, streaming the events for those unable to attend in person. Christmas season 2015–16 is shown here. *Parish Archives.*

Opposite, top: Kindergarten angels from the 2015 Advent play. *Teri Watters photo.*

Opposite, bottom: Kindergarten Wise Men from the 2015 Advent play. *Teri Watters photo.*

ST. CECILIA SCHOOL: FACTS AND FIGURES

- *The class of 1966 included fifty-five girls and forty-seven boys. About half of the boys went on to high school at St. Ignatius, with the rest about evenly divided between Sacred Heart and Riordan. Among the girls, fully half went on to Mercy—San Francisco, with the rest divided among the many other Catholic girls' schools of the day, including St. Rose, Star of the Sea, Presentation, Convent of the Sacred Heart and Notre Dame des Victoires.*
- *The class of 2015 included seventy students, again with girls having a slight edge in head count. With coeducation available in many Catholic high schools, well over half the class opted for either St. Ignatius (twenty-seven)*

or Sacred Heart Cathedral (twenty-three). Others chose Archbishop Riordan (seven) and Convent of the Sacred Heart (four), while the remainder of the class selected Mercy-Burlingame, Sacred Heart Schools—Atherton or one of the many fine public high schools in San Francisco or San Mateo Counties.

Faculty Reminiscences

St. Cecilia Parish has been blessed by the countless hours of personal sacrifice from the vowed religious women who have been members of the Sisters of the Holy Names of Jesus and Mary. The order received many young applicants who were graduates of St. Cecilia School, whose vocations to a religious calling were inspired while being taught by an earlier generation of nuns. Although teaching was a primary mission of this order ever since it was founded in 1843, many of the Sisters now provide support to other ministries beyond the classroom. Here are some memories of just a few of the hundreds of devoted women and men, both religious and lay, who have served our parish school well and faithfully over the years.

Former principals Sister Michaeline Falvey (who served from 1957 to 1962) and Sister Marilyn Miller (who served from 1992 to 2012) in December 2015. *Courtesy Sister Marilyn Miller.*

Sister Michaeline Falvey (Sister Michaeline Mary)

"In August of 1951, I was assigned to St. Cecilia School and spent my first few years teaching *sixty* 8th Grade boys at a time when the school had well over 800 students. The junior high classes were separated into boys and girls in those days, and I thoroughly enjoyed the challenge of dealing with a classroom full of lively boys—it was always an adventure!

"Even now, I'm still a big sports fan, and I encouraged my students by attending many of their games. Every day, I would walk the junior high boys across 19th Avenue to have lunch recess at Larsen Park, thus freeing up a very crowded schoolyard for the girls and for the children in the lower grades.

"After a few years the junior high classes became coed and the boys and girls were back together in the classroom the way they always were in their younger years. During the last six years of my time at St. Cecilia, I served as Principal of the school and also as Sister Superior at the convent—two very different hats, to be sure. In those days, most of the teachers were nuns, and each school year, we had many young women who were in the classroom for the very first time. I thoroughly enjoyed mentoring them and sharing my experiences with all of them.

"My fondest memories are of the children, who were bright, caring and enthusiastic. Their parents were very supportive and involved in both the school and the parish. I also loved working with the school secretary at the time, Marie Stanley. Mrs. Stanley, who would likely be called an Administrative Assistant today, was always gracious and welcoming to the school children, their parents and visitors. She was an enormous support to all of us during those years.

"Monsignor Collins, who was very committed to the parish, the school and his 'little pigeons,' was quite the character. I recall how he would ride in on a fire engine to begin the Christmas season and herald the grand opening of 18th Avenue between Vicente and Wawona, where families decorated the outside of their homes for all to see. Monsignor paid me a tremendous compliment when he lobbied with the SNJM community to allow me to remain at St. Cecilia School well beyond the usual six-year stay. He was well known for sending 'surprise' deliveries of Blum's incredible baked goods and candies to the convent to help us celebrate a Sister's birthday or feast day.

"Not many people know that we sisters used to have a few fun 'days off' on weekends during the school year. One of our favorite activities was going to Bean Hollow (an obscure beach on Highway 1) where we could all enjoy the beach and a picnic, thanks to some generous parishioners who 'lent us their station wagons for the trip. Some students wondered on Monday morning why so many of the Sisters had red faces!

"One of my biggest challenges was in 1962 when an assignment came for me to move on to another ministry, leaving my beloved St. Cecilia School, which happened to be my last assignment at the elementary school level.

"Even today, well into my retirement years, I am grateful for the many lifelong friendships that have been forged with students and parents—and I continue looking forward to attending as many class reunions as possible!"

Sister Marilyn Murphy (Sister Andrew Marie)

Sister Marilyn Murphy entered the fullness of life on April 18, 2014. She was eighty-four years old and celebrated fifty-seven years of religious profession as a Sister of the Holy Names of Jesus and Mary.

Sister Marilyn Murphy began her Easter celebration early as she joined the Kingdom of Heaven. There was much rejoicing and Easter Alleluias as she rejoined her parents, brother and many others of the Maginnis clan.

Sister Marilyn's ministry in elementary education took her to many places, including twenty years at St. Cecilia School in San Francisco, where she served as principal from the late 1970s until the 1990s, as well as an earlier assignment teaching sixth and seventh grades in the late 1950s and early 1960s as Sister Andrew Marie.

We remember Sister Marilyn's quiet, gentle and wise presence. We celebrate her profound goodness, understated humor, prayerfulness and keen sense of observation.

From website of the Sisters of the Holy Names of Jesus and Mary. Reprinted with permission.

Sister Shirley Sexton (Sister Maureen Theresa)

"I have competed well: I have finished the race: I have kept the faith."—2 Timothy 4:7

It is fitting that on May 16, 2015, the day before the Bay to Breakers, Sister Shirley finished her earthly race and was welcomed joyously by our God to the finish line. Sister Shirley was eighty-four years old and was celebrating her sixtieth year of profession as a Sister of the Holy Names of Jesus and Mary.

Sister Shirley was an elementary school educator, teaching eighth grade at Saint Cecilia (San Francisco) from 1961 to 1968. She also served as both a teacher and as principal at a number of other California schools before becoming a beloved director of residents at Holy Names University for four years.

While Sister Shirley's vibrancy and kindness drew others to her—from elementary school students to residents at HNU—these gifts of hers were a perfect fit for ministry with the elderly for over twenty years. She loved working with seniors, and she did so at Sacred Heart Parish, Saint Mary Center, Strawberry Creek Lodge, North Oakland Senior Center and Oakland Adult School. Her ministry to seniors always included the annual retreat at either Villa Maria Del Mar (Santa Cruz) or Villa Los Gatos. In all her ministries, Sister Shirley created in her heart a place of welcome and hospitality for whomever she met.

From the website of the Sisters of the Holy Names of Jesus and Mary. Reprinted with permission.

Sister Helen Walsh (Sister Mary Concilia)

Sister Helen Walsh was ninety-three years young when she was called home to God. She led a life of beautiful simplicity, gentleness and loving service mixed with a strong determination.

Sister Helen spent many years at St. Cecilia's School in San Francisco beginning in the late '70s, first as a reading teacher to those students who needed extra help and later as the first computer teacher to small groups of students. These students always looked forward to these classes. As time went on, Sister Helen moved from school ministry to parish ministry at St. Cecilia's. Again I quote from her biography:

> *As a religious, I spent many years teaching the faith to children in the classroom and growing in my faith and love of the Lord and marveling about the faith that keeps growing more precious every day.*
>
> *However, my years at St. Cecilia's Parish have been most enlightening. I have the privilege of bringing Holy Communion to shut-ins and speaking of Christ to them about the gospel I read to them in preparation. The more I speak of Christ to others, the more my faith and my love in Him grows. I also had the privilege of belonging to a group who came together to study*

the gospels (the Good News) each month so that they may grow in the knowledge of Jesus, the Author and Founder of the Faith that is ours.

Sister Helen's gentle, loving presence was a welcoming gift to all those she came in contact with. Many of the parishioners still speak lovingly of her today. The following is a short reflection from Sister Patti Doyle on the goodness of Sister Helen:

> *Sister Helen Walsh brought communion (on her bike!) to our Dad almost all of the four and a half years he lived after his stroke. She usually came early so she and Mom could have a little visit before Dad woke from his nap. I will never forget Sister Helen's gentle kindness to Mom well after Daddy died. Sister Helen continued to visit Mom just to see how she was doing.*
>
> *I understand this was pretty typical of Sister Helen's ministry with many others. I have no doubt she was welcomed into heaven by hundreds of men and women whom she helped get ready for their passing over the years. Bless you, dear Sister Helen!*

From the website of the Sisters of the Holy Names of Jesus and Mary. Reprinted with permission.

ST. CECILIA SCHOOL: FACTS AND FIGURES

- *For the school's first fifteen years, 1930 through 1945, all the teachers were Sisters of the Holy Names of Jesus and Mary, who were given new assignments by their order every few years. From 1946 through the late 1960s, several lay teachers began to join the faculty—at first, primarily older women who had already raised families—including Mrs. Mary Fitzpatrick, who taught kindergarten for many years in the 1940s and 1950s, as well as Mrs. Marie Tobin, who taught in both fourth grade and later fifth grade in the 1950s and 1960s. Beginning with Miss Pat Pinnick, who was hired in the mid-1950s, the lay faculty began to evolve into a group of career professionals, often hired just out of college, who remained on the job for longer periods of time than most of their predecessors, thus providing the school with an added level of experience and stability. Today, faculty members possess teaching credentials, several have completed master's degree programs and many have served in the classroom for twenty, thirty or forty years.*

- *In keeping with the changing world environment, school counselors now work with classroom teachers to provide conflict resolution programs for Grades K through 8, Smart Kids/Safe Kids for Grades K through 8, Safe Child education for Grades K through 3, a violence prevention program for Grade 6 and Project Choice (sponsored by the National Council on Alcoholism and other Drug Addictions) for Grades 4 through 8.*

Mrs. Claire Strehl

In the summer of 1946, in the interim between the death of Father John Harnett and just prior to the appointment of Monsignor Harold Collins as pastor, it became clear that there would soon be a gap in the teaching staff at St. Cecilia School.

Since the school first opened in the 1930–31 school year, the faculty had been 100 percent vowed religious from the Sisters of the Holy Names of Jesus and Mary. In the new post–World War II era, however, many things were changing, and religious orders were beginning to experience the beginnings of a gradual decline in young women becoming nuns. Also, with the new wing of the school being planned, the need for teachers was going to double beginning with the 1947–48 school year, and the Sisters of the Holy Names were beginning to take on additional ministries beyond elementary education, thus limiting the number of Sisters available for the classroom.

It was into these circumstances that Mrs. Claire Strehl, a longtime parishioner living on 14th Avenue near Vicente who had been a substitute teacher at St. Cecilia School since 1943, became the first permanent lay teacher in September 1946. As the mother of two girls, Mrs. Strehl had no problems in taking on a classroom full of lively sixth graders. A graduate of the old St. Rose Academy and UC Berkeley (class of 1928), Mrs. Strehl taught at St. Cecilia School for two years before being recruited to help with the opening of the new St. Gabriel School at 40th Avenue and Ulloa Street, which opened in 1948. She made the move and remained there for twenty-five years until her 1972 retirement at age sixty-five.

When she passed away in 2001 at the age of ninety-four at Nazareth House in San Rafael, Mrs. Strehl was fondly remembered in her *San Francisco Chronicle* obituary as being one of the first lay teachers in the San Francisco parochial school system.

Miss Patricia Pinnick

Pat Pinnick grew up in Epiphany Parish in San Francisco and graduated from the old Presentation High School at Turk and Masonic. She then went on to earn her bachelor's degree at Holy Names College (now University) in Oakland and began teaching sixth grade at St. Cecilia School in the fall of 1955.

Always adaptable, she taught fourth, fifth and sixth grades at various times during the early years of her long career before finally settling into third grade in the 1988–89 school year and remaining there until her retirement in 2005.

Recalling the various societal changes that took place during her long career, Pat remembered the challenges of explaining to a classroom of impressionable youngsters several extraordinary world events, such as assassinations of public figures, the deaths of two popes within a matter of weeks, the city hall murders in San Francisco, the tragedy of Peoples Temple in Guyana, the loss of the space shuttle *Challenger* and the 9/11 attacks on America. "These were the things that teachers were never taught in college, but after years in the classroom, you just develop a certain knack for conveying serious messages in ways that are age-appropriate for each grade level, so that the children will understand and be able to deal with the many different issues that they will encounter later in their lives."

At the time of her retirement from St. Cecilia School in 2005, after a teaching career of forty-nine years, Pat Pinnick (second from left) poses with other faculty members Kathy Kays (left), Principal Sister Marilyn Miller (second from right) and Marian Connelly (far right). Pat's three co-workers were also her students in earlier years. *Pinnick family photo.*

Speaking at a class reunion in 2010, Pat looked back fondly at her long career of forty-nine years teaching at St. Cecilia School. She recalled the sense of pleasure that she felt when new students came to her each September and confided, "Oh, Miss Pinnick, I'm so glad to be in your class because you taught my sister/brother." She admitted to being a just bit startled when, what seemed like just a few years later, the message had changed to, "Oh, Miss Pinnick, I'm so glad to be in your class because you taught my mother/father." Still, such comments conveyed a pleasant sense of continuity and community. Pat admitted to being truly shocked, however, when a student came to her at the turn of the millennium and said, "Oh, Miss Pinnick, I'm so glad to be in your class because you taught my *grandfather!*" Pat admitted wryly, "It was about then that I began to think a bit more seriously about the possibility of retirement."

Even after her record-breaking forty-nine-year teaching stint at St. Cecilia School, Miss Pinnick did not remain away from elementary education for long. In the fall of 2005, during her first months of retirement, she learned that nearby St. Thomas More School needed a long-term, part-time substitute teacher for its third grade. Pat stepped in to fill the role and eventually stayed on to become the school's librarian, a position she held until January 2015, when she went to be with the Lord, following more than sixty years of devoted service to the children of our community.

Mr. Tom Kennedy

"My history in San Francisco was very traditional. I spent my early years in Epiphany Parish. We moved to St. Cecilia's when I was entering 1st Grade in the Fall of 1951. My father was an officer with the San Francisco Police Department and my mother a secretary. My older brother graduated from St. Cecilia's as well. I then went to Saint Ignatius and University of Santa Clara. I received my Teaching Credential and my Master's Degree in Education from USF.

"In the Spring of 1967, I was completing my senior year at the University of Santa Clara. It was then that I was contacted by St. Cecilia's to see if I had any interest in coming on board as a teacher. Half the student body was male and there was obviously some thought given to having a male teacher. There were already many great male coaches but no male teachers. Personally, I had a tremendous interest in a teaching-coaching career. Coming onto the staff at St. Cecilia's allowed me to take a position as a football coach at Riordan High School as well. This became an extraordinarily busy time because I was teaching at St. Cecilia's, coaching at Riordan and going to USF at night for my Teaching Credential.

"Stepping into a 6th Grade classroom for the first time is a humbling experience. I had three unbelievable mentors: Sister Mary of St. John (later known as Sister Claire Duggan), Principal, plus Sister Maureen Theresa (aka Sister Shirley Sexton) and Sister Eileen Catharine (aka Sister Kathleen

McDonough), who were the two eighth grade teachers—in fact, Sister Eileen Catharine had been my eighth grade teacher at St. Cecilia's. The three of them kept me grounded and added a much needed sense of humor at critical periods.

"A new eighth grade science module was put into the curriculum for the 1967 school year. The Diocese held two Saturday training sessions for the teachers involved so they would know how to conduct the science demonstrations in the classroom. Since I was coaching at Riordan, I was busy on Saturdays and could not make the training. Sister Eileen Catharine, who was also teaching the science module, used to train me on the demonstrations in the morning before class. It's a wonder I didn't cause any damage in the classroom!

"The kids were amazing. I am always so impressed by the foundation they brought with them to 6th Grade from their previous years at St. Cecilia's. They were smart, articulate, energetic and willing to learn. In fact, over my two years there, I only had to kick one boy out of the classroom.

"The beginning of the school year was a new experience for these 50 students. It was dead silence and strict attention because they had no idea what to do with a man in front of them. However, just as with their parents, they would test to see what the limits were. My most infamous classroom experience, and the one people remind me of today when I see them, concerns my watch. One day, I thought the kids were making too much noise. Rather than ask for quiet, I slammed my hand on the desk to startle them. I hit the desk so hard my watch exploded—needless to say they still enjoy that to this day.

"I taught at St. Cecilia's for two years. In the summer before my second year I was married in Santa Cruz. Some of my 6th Grade students came down to the wedding. That meant a lot to me that they had an interest. My two years went by very quickly. The students were fun and each had a different personality and different dreams. Some of them I later taught and coached at St. Ignatius as well. It's really amazing to run into them now and hear about their lives and families. They have done very well.

"I taught at Saint Ignatius for four years before deciding to leave teaching and coaching. I then went to work for Clementina Equipment Rentals. That got me into the Construction Equipment Rental industry which is where I spent my entire career. During that period, my wife and I moved from Petaluma back to San Francisco and into the parish, and our two daughters graduated from St. Cecilia School. I held myriad positions in the Rental Industry from Outside Sales to District Manager and onto Vice President of Operations before I retired in 2010.

"Teaching definitely helps you for work in other careers. I never had a fear of standing in front of a group and making a presentation. If you can do it in front of a group of fifty 6th Graders, you can do it in front of anybody."

Mrs. Catherine Ring

In the winter of 1963, a young woman from a small farm in Ireland came to St. Cecilia to interview for a teaching position. It was her last interview, as she was hired for the job and would serve as a teacher, vice-principal, First Communion coordinator, mentor and friend to thousands of parishioners for the next thirty-three years.

Catherine Kelleher was born in County Cork, Ireland, in 1934 and came to America on a boat that departed from the seaport town of Cobh when she was just sixteen years old. After first arriving in New Orleans, she made her way west in 1952. She found a home in San Francisco with relatives who had settled in the city a generation earlier, and she completed her high school education at St. Paul's in Noe Valley. She eventually started teaching for a brief time at St. James School and St. Monica School, met John Ring at the Knights of the Red Branch—a popular Irish social club known as the KRB—and then married and started a family.

Catherine was known for many things at St. Cecilia. She was a Grade 3 teacher initially, yet is most fondly remembered for her work in Grade 2/ Room 3, where she taught her students how to read and sing and prepared them for First Communion. She was tough but fair, and she was the last of a generation that used a wooden clapper, just like the nuns, to keep order and discipline in the classroom. It has been said that the same sharp, biting sound from the clapper that sent fear into the hearts of eight-year-olds throughout the 1960s, 1970s and 1980s could probably still silence an adult crowd in a packed West Portal bar on a Saturday night.

Despite the fact that she built her reputation on discipline, Catherine Ring was very funny. She was well known for entertaining her colleagues in the faculty room with a variety of interesting stories that cannot be repeated here. Outside her family, those closest to Catherine were the people she met through her work at St. Cecilia—longtime secretary Margaret Carberry; parent Mary Chang; teachers Fran Cavanagh, Sister Margaret Kinzie, Sheila Hood, Joan Leehane and Carolyn Daley; teacher aides Mary Greene, Mary McKeon and Noreen McNamara; and scores of others.

End-of-school-year celebration in 2002, with faculty members (left to right) Mrs. Catherine Ring, Ms. Fran Cavanagh, Miss Carolyn Daley and Sister Marilyn Murphy. *Courtesy Fran Cavanagh.*

Although Catherine passed away suddenly just a few years after her 1996 retirement, her connection to the school she loved remains strong. Four of her grandchildren (Kieran Firlit-Ring, Katie Hagan, Eddie Hagan and Hope Hagan) graduated from St. Cecilia School in recent years, and five others (Elizabeth Ring, Sean Haettenschwiller, Aidan Ring, Tara Hagan and Kyle Haettenschwiller) are attending now and will be SC graduates one day if they manage to stay out of trouble.

Catherine Ring was proud to work at St. Cecilia, and she certainly took to heart Monsignor Collins's idea of being "the Finest, the Greatest, and the Best." She had high expectations for herself, her students and the school as a whole, and it showed in her work and her treatment of others.

On behalf of Catherine, the Ring family sends best wishes to St. Cecilia Parish on the occasion of its 100th anniversary.

Submitted by Catherine's children: Mary Ellen (MER) Ring ('77), Annette Hagan ('80) and John Ring ('82).

Mrs. Marian Mulkerrins Connelly

"Since 1967, I have been a part of this school—initially as a student; then as a volunteer during my high school and college years; later as a teacher, member of the leadership team and a vice-principal; and currently as the school's first lay principal.

"There are so many events that build community at St. Cecilia—the Sunday 9:30 a.m. Family Mass, the annual parish picnic, Parish Festival, Mothers' Club fundraiser, St. Patrick's Dinner and Men of St. Cecilia Club Crab Feed to name a few. For me, working at St. Cecilia is much more than a job; it has been a significant part of my life for almost 50 years. I cherish the relationships that I have formed over the years with clergy, faculty, staff, parents and students, and I honor the fine history and traditions of our school, plus the charism of the Sisters of the Holy Names of Jesus and Mary."

Mrs. Teri DeBenedetti Watters

"Being in the right place at the right time led me back to St. Cecilia School. It was 1972, and I was a USF student, coaching a St. Cecilia kickball team. Sister Sylvia, the principal at that time, walked through the schoolyard one afternoon and asked what my class hours were at USF and then hired me on the spot to be an aide in First and Second Grades. Groomed by Catherine Ring, Sister Agatha Rose, Carolyn Daley and Maureen Mostyn-Brown, I then became a teacher assigned to 3rd Grade for 10 years before moving to my permanent home in Kindergarten where I have been since the Fall of 1986. My husband and I sent our four children to St. Cecilia School, where they were educated and nurtured by the Sisters of the Holy Names and by many dedicated lay faculty and friends. St. Cecilia has a fabulous community filled with wonderful children and their families. Now to be teaching the children of the children I taught years ago is so rewarding. St. Cecilia has been a part of our family for many years, since my siblings and I were students here, and with our son Chris now also teaching here, it will continue to be so for many years to come."

ST. CECILIA PARISH IN THE NEWS

On a dark and windy night in February 2002, the gold cross surmounting the Spanish-tiled dome on the steeple of St. Cecilia Church came crashing to the ground, embedding itself in the concrete plaza in front of the church entrance. Thankfully, no one was injured, and research quickly revealed that over the previous forty-six years, the area's salty fogs had eroded the base of the cross, as a result of inadequate sealing during construction, causing it to fall. Repairs were quickly undertaken—at a cost of more than $10,000—and the cross was restored to the top of the dome, where it remains a neighborhood icon. The message was clear, though: buildings require periodic—and sometimes costly—maintenance.

BY THE NUMBERS

One of the most dramatic changes in the parish over the years is the number of active parishioners. Although head count has declined, this change has brought about new opportunities for volunteerism that did not exist in earlier days. Lay lectors, parishioners presenting the gifts during Mass, classroom aides, student service hours and many other changes have brought about greater involvement of all parishioners in the daily life of the community. The author is grateful to parish secretary Mary Scanlon for researching the many facts and figures included in this section.

School Attendance

One of the changes that began several decades ago involves the reduction of class size at St. Cecilia School. From a high of 886 students in the 1952–53 school year, the figure dropped to 800 when kindergarten was eliminated in 1957 and remained steady for more than a full decade. The elimination of kindergarten was necessitated by archdiocesan guidelines limiting class size and also by San Francisco Fire Department regulations concerning the school's safety capacity. By 1980, when kindergarten was first reinstated, overall attendance was lower, primarily due to lower birthrates and higher tuition costs (reflecting the increased expenses of a nearly 100 percent lay teaching staff). The upside was that the school now has an average class size of 30 to 35 students (versus 50 per classroom in the peak years and 60 per classroom prior to the 1948 expansion).

Baptisms

During the years of the post–World War II baby boom (1946–64), it was not uncommon to have half a dozen or more baptisms scheduled for a Sunday afternoon. The declining birthrate, the draw of suburban living and the dramatic increase in housing prices in San Francisco have all been cited as factors that have contributed to a reduced number of children living in the parish over the last several decades.

Marriages

Again, this is a statistic controlled largely by the number of young people in the parish community. In the decade of the 1950s, there were 464 marriages. Excluding the six weeks of Lent and the four weeks of Advent, when the church itself is in a time of penance and prayerful contemplation of upcoming ecclesiastical events and does not ordinarily schedule weddings, these 464 marriages were spread over about forty Saturdays per year. Thus, there was an average of more than one wedding per weekend—often 2 or 3 on Saturdays in the popular months of May and June.

By the decade of the 1960s, there were 420 marriages—still an average of 1 wedding per weekend, usually with multiple ceremonies on Saturdays in May and June. The decline, however, was on by the late 1960s. Numbers continued to drop gradually for the remainder of the twentieth century, and from 2000 to 2014, there were only 334 weddings, an average of just over 2 per month for that fifteen-year period. In 2015, the full-year total was just 14 weddings—barely 1 per month—and this number continues to decline, as the parish has fewer and fewer single members in the twenty-five to thirty-five age group.

And while all weddings are special—more than two thousand brides and grooms have been down the aisle of St. Cecilia Church since 1956, celebrating their new lives together—sometimes these events have special meaning to the entire parish.

In October 2010, the St. Cecilia class of 1960 held a reunion in honor of the fifty years since graduation. It was during that event that Robert Hurrell and Maureen McCarthy, classmates from kindergarten through eighth grade, saw each other and had a chance to reconnect—each of them was then single after the loss of a longtime spouse. It was a busy weekend, including a Friday night reception in the Collins Center, a Saturday night dinner at the United Irish Cultural Center and Sunday Mass at St. Cecilia Church, followed by a farewell brunch.

Bob and Maureen kept in touch after that reunion, and much to the surprise of their classmates, the couple soon announced their engagement. On July 12, 2014, they were married in St. Cecilia Church, with Maureen's mother, still hale and hearty in her nineties, escorting her daughter down the aisle, along with Maureen's brother, Father Michael McCarthy, SJ, who then switched roles and performed the Nuptial Mass. At the offertory, a contingent of more than twenty of the couple's classmates from their 1960 graduating class processed down the aisle, presenting gifts of bread and wine at the altar.

In the words of one of the classmate guests: "How often can you combine a very happy wedding with a class reunion? Maureen and Bob could not have been more gracious and generous hosts, and it was very special for all of us to see the amazing river of life that started in kindergarten and has brought us over time back together to see this day, seeing those two five-year-olds in our first group photo from the fall of 1951, now more mature, pledging their lives together for the balance of their journey here on earth."

Ministry for the Sick: Father Heribert Duquet, 1914–2013

Born in France in July 1914 just before the start of World War I, Father Heribert Duquet was ordained in Paris in 1939, just prior to the start of World War II. From 1940 to 1945, he was a prisoner of war in Germany. Upon his release, he returned to missionary service in Singapore, Canada and the United States.

From 1977 to 2002, he acted as an assistant in St. Cecilia Parish in San Francisco. His appointment came at a time when the pastor, Monsignor McKay, noted the changing needs of a very large number of parishioners who had become senior citizens. Father Duquet soon began a devoted ministry to the sick and elderly parishioners. His handwritten journals, still maintained in the rectory, reflect the names of the hundreds of women and men he visited each week, often taking Holy Communion to fifty or more parishioners (including the author's own mother from 1992 to 2002) while visiting homes and apartments throughout the parish, as well as nursing homes in San Francisco and northern San Mateo County. Finally in 2002, after twenty-five years of service to the family of St. Cecilia Parish, "Pere" (as Father was affectionately called) retired permanently to St. Anne's Home on Lake Street, where the Little Sisters of the Poor took exceptional care of him until he went to be with the Lord eleven years later, in 2013, when he was nearly ninety-nine years old. He will be remembered in a special way for his priestly service to the sick and dying, the twinkle in his eyes and his deep love of the "Good Lord."

PERSONAL REMINISCENCE: FRANK DUNNIGAN

After she turned eighty years old in 1994, Mom found it increasingly difficult to navigate the stairs in her home, and although she was able to continue living fairly independently, she began going out far less frequently. For nearly ten years before her death, Father Duquet brought Holy Communion to her every Tuesday afternoon. Like many of those who had been taught by Catholic nuns in the 1930s, Mom wanted to be ready for his visit with all the requirements that she remembered from the old days—including meeting the priest at the door silently with a lighted candle and having the never-used "sick call crucifix" from her bedroom wall set up on the coffee table with two lighted beeswax candles, plus a linen cloth and holy water. Father Duquet was very nice, assuring her that they only needed a place to sit down. As more and more of her neighbors became housebound and began to rely on Father Duquet's weekly visits, Mom fielded phone calls from many of her friends with the pressing question: "Katherine, what am I supposed to do when the priest brings me Holy Communion here at home?"

Funerals and Memorial Services

For many years, it was clear that St. Cecilia had a wide range of age groups among the parish family. Highlighting this fact were events ranging from multiple baptisms on Sunday afternoons to a seriously overcrowded elementary school, multiple weddings every weekend, Sunday Mass attendance of about five thousand people and, finally, the large number of funerals each and every week of the year.

There were 729 funerals held at St. Cecilia Church in the decade of the 1950s—about 1.5 per week, on average, every week for the entire decade. By the 1960s, the count was up to 976 for the decade—nearly 2 per week for a full ten years. Then a gradual reversal began, so that there were only 1,062 funerals during that entire fifteen-year period from 2000 to 2014—slightly over 1 per week.

Each and every year, we say goodbye to fifty or more members of the St. Cecilia Parish community and even more who were school alums or former parishioners—people who have loved and served the Lord faithfully. Some of these friends depart after long, healthy lives lived out over many decades, while some have experienced the challenges of ill health. Others leave us suddenly, sometimes far sooner than expected, heeding God's call that their time on earth has reached a conclusion.

These were the people who supported the Mothers' Club, the Knights of St. Cecilia, the League of the Sacred Heart and other organizations for decades. They were student leaders, ran the festivals, volunteered for school events and presented the gifts at Mass. They took up the Sunday collections, worked as lectors and altar servers, volunteered for parish picnics and retreats, sometimes taught in the school for decades and generously offered their support to the parish family in countless other ways. Sometimes they were called home to God abruptly and without warning—serving to remind us all that our own time here on earth is limited.

Funerals and memorial services today can take many different forms. Some families prefer the quiet intimacy of a family-only Mass or other service in Our Lady's Chapel, while larger gatherings often fill the church itself to overflowing. Music might range from traditional organ selections to contemporary guitar music to somber mariachi melodies or mournful bagpipes, all reflecting a variety of cultures and traditions.

Favorite songs are chosen— from "The Beer Barrel Polka" at

Dot Mazza

March 28th, 1925
March 21st, 1998

St. Cecilia's Church
San Francisco
March 25th, 1998

Program for the 1998 Funeral Mass of a longtime parishioner. *Courtesy Nancy Mazza.*

Monsignor Collins's 1980 funeral to "Danny Boy," which was played at the Funeral Mass for the author's father. "Amazing Grace," "When the Saints Go Marching In" and "On Eagle's Wings" all represent popular contemporary religious music, while the "Ave Maria," sung in Latin, is a regular request at many services. On one extraordinarily sad occasion in 1989, "Surfer Girl" was played and sung for a beloved 1966 graduate of the school—a successful singer-musician whose life was ended by a tragic auto accident.

Often, following the services, the family may host a reception for relatives and friends at home or, in the case of larger events, at the Durocher Pavilion. Food and fellowship have long conveyed strong human emotions, and even today, any announcement of a death within the parish community sets many people to work helping to prepare a post-funeral gathering for the deceased's loved ones.

This author's own mother was well known for always having a large covered Pyrex dish with a Campbell's soup–based casserole readily at hand in her freezer, "so that I can send a nice hot dish in case someone dies." In her later years, Mom found herself sending and then replenishing that prepared Pyrex dish more and more frequently for the families of our friends and neighbors. Today, such kitchen offerings also include lumpia, pakoras and egg rolls just as often as lasagna, soda bread, casseroles and biscotti, but the message remains the same. We offer our companionship and comfort to the bereaved through gifts of food for the body and prayers for the souls of the departed, as well as for the emotional and the spiritual well-being of loved ones who remain behind. These are some of the things we do for one another as a family.

Although the number of funerals remains lower than in previous times, a large number of families today are choosing to return to St. Cecilia Church to hold final services for family members who were once active parishioners. This sense of "coming home" to the familiar surroundings of St. Cecilia Church and its parish community has been cited by many as being an important part of the healing process for their own personal grief at the loss of a parent or other loved one.

Mass Attendance

Catholic churches have traditionally monitored head counts at Sunday Mass. Particularly after the relaxation of rules in the early 1950s regarding fasting before Holy Communion, it became easier for the faithful to partake in the Eucharist on a regular basis. By then, it was estimated that many more Sunday Mass attendees were receiving Communion on a weekly basis. Prior to this, fasting was required after midnight, so that relatively few Sunday Mass attendees were receiving Communion weekly—and hardly any at the 12:15 p.m. Mass, when a thirteen-hour fast, including no water, would have been required by the time of Communion.

During most of the 1950s and 1960s, Sunday Mass attendance at St. Cecilia Church was over five thousand persons per week. Even when Saturday Vigil attendance was counted beginning in the early 1970s, an overall decline in weekly Mass attendance was noted; it had become more pronounced by the end of the millennium, when weekly attendance settled at the level of about two thousand persons. The changes in the Sunday Mass schedule clearly reflect this:

Father Patrick Summerhays, pastor Monsignor Michael Harriman and school principal Mrs. Marian Connelly at the 2015 "Wild, Wild West" Parish Festival. For nearly seventy years, the annual festival has been one of the primary fundraisers held to benefit the school. *Courtesy Donagh McKeown.*

1970 WEEKEND MASS SCHEDULE

5:30 p.m.	Saturday vigil—Upper Church only
6:30 a.m.	Upper Church only
8:00 a.m.	Upper Church only
9:00 a.m.	Upper and Lower Church
10:00 a.m.	Upper and Lower Church
11:00 a.m.	Upper Church only (High Mass)
12:15 p.m.	Upper and Lower Church

2016 WEEKEND MASS SCHEDULE

5:00 p.m.	Saturday vigil—Upper Church only
7:30 a.m.	Upper Church only
9:30 a.m.	Upper Church only
11:30 a.m.	Upper Church only

PERSONAL REMINISCENCE: FATHER PATRICK SUMMERHAYS

After graduating from USF's MBA program in 1998, I was hired as a financial analyst for a biotech start-up firm here in San Francisco. The company merged several previously independent operations throughout the world and quickly became the largest radiology service company to the pharmaceutical research industry, helping develop drugs to combat debilitating diseases such as osteoporosis, arthritis, cancer and Alzheimer's.

I later moved to Phoenix and transitioned from corporate finance into personal finance, selling insurance and investments to private individuals. I really enjoyed spending increased time with people, discussing life and retirement goals. While working with some Catholic clients, our shared faith often would become a topic of conversation. Ultimately, I began to see that there was a desire in my heart to move beyond the material goals and aspirations of wealth management. I discovered that these conversations related to the Catholic faith were always the most meaningful. Slowly, God was calling me away from spreadsheets and investment prospectuses.

In truth, various priests had encouraged me to think about the Catholic priesthood throughout my adult life. Finally, my parish pastor in Phoenix recognized this calling and asked me to be open to it. It took me several months after he broached the topic before I began to see a priestly calling for myself, and in 2006, I began studying at St. John Vianney Seminary in Denver to be a priest for the Diocese of Phoenix. While attending the seminary there, I began to sense a call back to San Francisco. So, in 2010, I returned to the Bay Area and entered St. Patrick's Seminary for the Archdiocese of San Francisco.

My friends, family and co-workers were very supportive of this decision. Some were less comfortable, and they had their probing questions. But generally, everyone respected this decision and remained encouraging.

Right after the ordination Mass, Archbishop Cordileone informed me that I would be assigned to St. Cecilia Parish. I was initially surprised because I had convinced myself that I would be assigned somewhere on the peninsula, but I was excited for the opportunity to share in the storied history here. I had come to know St. Cecilia's while I lived and worked in San Francisco. I even attended Masses here on Saturdays and Sundays in the late 1990s. I always found St. Cecilia to be one of the most beautiful churches in San Francisco, and ironically, I thought, "If I have the choice someday, St. Cecilia would be my choice of any city church to be married in." Hah—God had his own plan, and he got me to the altar another way!

Above: On February 26, 2012, Monsignor Harriman was given a surprise seventieth birthday party in the lower church. *Jorge Guerzon photo.*

Left: In May 2008, the parish celebrated the fortieth anniversary of Monsignor Harriman's ordination to the priesthood. *Jorge Guerzon photo.*

Above: The 2012 birthday party, hosted by the Filipino community and the Indonesian community of St. Cecilia Parish, acknowledged Monsignor Harriman as the second-longest-serving pastor. *Jorge Guerzon photo.*

Right: As St. Cecilia Parish begins its second century of service to the people of San Francisco, the 1956 church building continues to exude a sense of stability and community across the entire neighborhood, more than sixty years after its dedication. *Courtesy Mary Ellen (MER) Ring.*

ST. CECILIA PARISH IN THE NEWS

STEWARDSHIP
From the March 2016 issue of the parish newsletter:

As our parish community continues to grow and develop stewardship as a way of life, we will focus on what's going on in the St. Cecilia community, and how those activities and events are changing hearts and minds and helping parishioners grow closer to Christ and each other. Our hope is that the new parish newsletter will be a successful means for ongoing education and formation in our faith, and I pray it will be a vehicle through which you are informed and inspired to become more actively involved in the life of Christ and the parish.

It is important to remember that stewardship is a way of life, and not a program. True Catholic stewardship involves an ongoing call to live as followers of Christ. It takes time to find and define personal goals. You can begin by examining your personal commitments to the parish. How do you live your faith in your daily life with your family and friends? How much time do you spend in daily prayer, going to Mass or being involved in parish ministries and activities? What percentage of your income should you give back to God every week? What talents do you have that could be used to strengthen our parish family?

The coming months will see us increasing and intensifying our education and communication on stewardship. We will be developing a better understanding of how stewardship is a way of responding to God's call to discipleship. And with God's help, changes will occur in each of our hearts as we devote ourselves to a stewardship renewal within our parish. Examine how you are currently responding to God's call to stewardship. If God called you home tomorrow, would He proclaim, "Well done, my good and faithful servant"?

As we strive to develop stewardship as a way of life at St. Cecilia, the support and involvement of each individual parishioner is necessary to sustain the life of our parish. All of you have a place here, and all of you have a role to fill in the life of the parish as we live our lives as disciples of Christ. May the Holy Spirit renew and refresh all of us as we work together to build our parish family through the use of our time, talent and treasure.

Sincerely yours in Christ,
Monsignor Michael D. Harriman

Chapter 8

LOOKING AHEAD

2017 and Beyond

In the course of compiling this book, I have become an avid reader of the weekly parish bulletin, the monthly parish newsletter and the school's weekly e-newsletter, plus monthly updates from the Centennial Committee. I continue to be amazed at the breadth and depth of programs now in place for everyone in the parish family. Recent announcements have included information on dozens of religious programs, social events and fundraisers, including:

- First Eucharist class, confirmation preparation, weekly baptisms and funerals, vespers and Benediction, Chinese Bible study, Legion of Mary, choir, lectors, altar servers, May Procession, student body Mass and Centennial events (anniversary Mass, dinner, photo exhibit, parish photo directory, memorial brick wall and parish history book).

- Language lessons (Chinese, French, Italian, Spanish), exercise, yoga and qi-gong groups, bingo, bridge, Scrabble, Pedro, knitting and crocheting, Young Families Group, Chinese Club potluck, Italian-Catholic Federation, Men of St. Cecilia maintenance events and after-Mass coffee and donuts.

- School library book donations; student body elections; sporting events and practices; school yearbook; spring musical; sandwiches for the hungry; girls' alumni basketball game; St. Cecilia–Holy Name sports

Members of the St. Cecilia class of 2009 gather at the Collins Center in 2013 after high school graduations are over and before going off to college. Today, many of them are graduating from college, and several will likely return to the neighborhood in the future to form the next generation of St. Cecilia parishioners. *Veronica Granucci photo.*

tournament; Mothers' Club fundraisers; class reunions for the classes of 1956, 1966, 1976 and 1996; and the annual fall festival.

St. Cecilia Parish in the News

In April 2016, Monsignor Harriman announced the beginning of a long-term project for the parish and school community. Following a seismic analysis of all schools undertaken by the Archdiocese of San Francisco, work is set to begin on planning retrofit projects that will strengthen school structures in order to increase life safety during future earthquakes. Parishioners are now becoming involved in developing a strategic plan for the project, with work estimated to be completed during the summer months over a period of two or three years.

Over the past twelve months, I have also spoken to and corresponded with hundreds of current and former St. Cecilia parishioners, students and faculty members. Some have had a longtime involvement with the parish, occasionally with an ancestor among the original fifty-nine families from 1917. Many more, though, came along in later years—part of the post–World War II baby boom or from even more recent times, including this new millennium. Many of those who have moved to other locales, myself included, still think of St. Cecilia Parish as "home."

One recurring theme that was repeated frequently by dozens of people from every generation and every background was gratitude for what they themselves had received during their time as part of the St. Cecilia Parish family. Many of those comments can be combined and summarized as follows:

> *Members of our family have clearly benefitted from the experience of membership in Catholic parishes and Catholic schools. My parents/ grandparents were people of modest means, and they often had to struggle, but the Catholic elementary and high schools over the years were frequently able to reduce or waive tuition because of the generosity of financial donors and volunteers from long ago.*
>
> *My parents were active in St. Cecilia Parish as a way of paying back all those who had gone before them—in fact, saying "thank you" to the Catholic community that had helped them in their early years to achieve some level of financial stability by adulthood. Both my mother and my father were dedicated to volunteering for many Catholic activities for the rest of their lives—St. Cecilia festivals, League of the Sacred Heart, coaching sports teams, fundraising for St. Mary's Hospital, Little Sisters of the Poor and Little Children's Aid, plus the Catholic high schools and colleges that my siblings and I attended, Catholic charities, CYO and many other organizations.*
>
> *If it weren't for the generosity of the many donors and volunteers from various times in the past, I would not be the person I am today— and this is the legacy of giving and volunteering that I want to pass on to members of my own family.*

As I look back exactly fifty years to my own graduation from St. Cecilia School in June 1966, I can echo these thoughts wholeheartedly. At a time when so many of my classmates are re-connecting with one another for the first time in half a century, we can all see examples of generosity and volunteerism in the lives of our friends—traits that were first nurtured by our parents, as well as by the priests, nuns, and lay faculty of St. Cecilia Parish so long ago.

To all the current and former members of this community who have contributed so much in terms of time, talent and treasure generously to our parish family over the past century, many thanks for your participation in the San Francisco parish that remains "the Finest, the Greatest and the Best."

Frank Dunnigan
June 2016

SOME RELIGIOUS VOCATIONS FROM THE PARISH

SISTER MARY ELLENE EGAN, RSM

Born in San Francisco, Ellene Marie Egan was the younger of the two children of James Egan, a San Francisco policeman, and Thelma Hennig Egan. She grew up near 19th Avenue and Taraval Street, attended St. Cecilia School (class of 1960) and Mercy High School–SF (class of 1964). She entered the Sisters of Mercy shortly after high school graduation and professed her vows in 1967. She earned her Bachelor of Arts degree at Russell College, an institution run by the Sister of Mercy in Burlingame. She went on to earn a Bachelor of Science degree in nursing from the University of San Francisco in 1971.

Upon graduation, Ellene went to work as a nursing supervisor at Mercy Hospital in San Diego, and in 1977, she enrolled in master's degree program at Loma Linda University, earning that degree in 1979. She then began a thirty-three-year career on the faculty of the University of San Francisco School of Nursing and Health Professions, teaching and coaching generations of student nurses in a profession that she truly loved. In 1989, she returned to the student side of the classroom, earning a doctorate in education from USF.

She also served as faculty chair of the School of Nursing, as treasurer to the USF Faculty Association and as board member of the California Nurses Association. In addition, she was chair of the St. Mary's Medical Center–San

Francisco Board of Directors and also a member of the Catholic Charities/ CYO Board of Directors.

Her volunteer work remained widespread throughout the Bay Area community. In 2004, she volunteered to take on the huge task of organizing the 150th anniversary celebration for the Sisters of Mercy at St. Mary's Cathedral. She was chosen to the leadership team of the order's Burlingame Regional Community in 2006 as the community was transitioning to become part of a new national organization. After much prayer and personal reflection about leaving her beloved USF for a time, she decided she was being called to do that.

In the last decade of her life, she was active in Most Holy Redeemer Parish (MHR) in San Francisco when another Sister called on her and invited her to join the parish's choir. Sister Ellene loved the parish and her involvement in it, serving on the MHR finance board, as a lector and on the search committee for a new choir director. She continued serving her community of the Sisters of Mercy as a member of Mercy High School–Burlingame Board of Directors and a member of the Sisters' Retirement Committee, as well as her term on the leadership team.

Ellene's active life was unexpectedly curtailed in June 2012 when she was diagnosed with cancer. She spent the last year undergoing treatment while residing at Marian Oaks, the Sisters' retirement center in Burlingame. Sister Ellene died in Burlingame at the relatively young age of sixty-six just one year later in June 2013. She was survived by an aunt, nephew, niece, grandnieces, other relatives and her beloved community of the Sisters of Mercy. Her Funeral Mass was offered by her St. Cecilia classmate from 1960, Father Michael Strange, and was attended by many of her former classmates from grammar school, high school and college, along with students and friends from her long and devoted life of giving to others.

Father Michael Strange

"I was born in 1939, graduated from St. Cecilia School in 1953, and then entered the seminary, with my ordination taking place in 1965.

"One of the focal points of my growing up in the Parkside, on 21st Avenue just south of Santiago, was the shopping excursions to the 22nd and Taraval Market, Baronial Bakery, Mrs. Corsiglia's Overland Pharmacy, the Miller Sisters' Ice Cream Shop and the Five-and-Dime where one could find any necessity. Attractions outside the immediate area that drew us were the Zoo, the DeYoung Museum, the Aquarium—all free—as well as Fleishhacker Pool, the biggest swimming pool in the world at the time, filled with heated salt water, right next to the Zoo—and back then, all of these amusements were free.

"At the core of our life, however, was St. Cecilia's. The social life of my parents, Arthur and Maleada Strange, revolved around the activities of the church and the school. Together with their closest friends, they led, worked on and celebrated every social event in the parish, as well as prayed and grew spiritually. As the youngest in my family, I tagged along to many meetings and setup events. The Church, spiritually and socially, was our center, and I am quite certain that my priestly vocation was nurtured in that special environment.

"In the Fall of 1945, I entered the first grade along with well over fifty others. As a second grader, on a usual foggy day, we welcomed our new pastor, Msgr. Harold E. Collins, who soon brought new life, expanding the school to a double class for each grade level and eventually building a magnificent church. We truly believed that we were the finest, the greatest and the best.

"I have many happy memories of my time at St. Cecilia's School with the wonderful Sisters of the Holy Names. After my ordination I had the privilege of staying at St. Cecilia's during my summer and Christmas breaks from seminary teaching in Seattle. I learned parish work from a master. I was welcomed back by people who knew me as a boy, and I appreciated all the recent parishioners who brought a renewed sense of vitality into the parish. I witnessed some of the struggles as both church and society changed and grew.

"In the 1990s, I had the privilege of teaching at a seminary in Zambia. One day some American Sisters visited us. One asked where I was from, and I replied, 'St. Cecilia's in San Francisco,' I replied. 'Oh, the finest, the greatest and the best,' she said. We were known worldwide!"

Note: Father Strange is in residence at St. Stephen's Parish.

SR. MARILYN MILLER, SNJM

"My family lived on 27th Avenue, between Ulloa and Vicente, and I graduated from St. Cecilia School in 1959 and then went to Mercy High School on 19th Avenue, where I graduated in 1963. I then entered the Sisters of the Holy Names and completed college while preparing for a career in elementary education.

"From 1989 to 1992 I was the Elementary Coordinator for schools in California that were staffed by Holy Names Sisters. I lived at St. Cecilia Convent and visited the school from 1989 to 1992 in that capacity. So I was familiar with that faculty and programs that were in place when I became Principal upon the retirement of Sister Marilyn Murphy in 1992.

"It must have been a challenge to the school staff to have had two Principals in a row, both named 'Sister Marilyn'—I'm told that among the teachers we were often referred to for clarity as 'old Marilyn' and 'new Marilyn.'

"Memories from my 20 years as Principal, from 1992 to 2012, remain very positive: providing a strong religious environment that helped to foster faith development, ministering in a positive environment where the school remains such an integral part of the parish community and also ministering with a pastor who was always so supportive. I thoroughly enjoyed working with parents and parishioners to plan and dedicate the school computer lab, the Durocher Pavilion, and two kindergarten classrooms.

"It was also a time of many spiritual and temporal challenges in our daily lives: trying to provide for the varying needs of all the students, increased challenges regarding school law, parental expectations and archdiocesan requirements, providing tuition assistance for needy families during difficult economic times and supporting the needs of the school and parish community at times when some students and parents were suddenly called home to God.

"Going forward, I am so pleased to see the current administration integrating technology into the curriculum, meeting needs of students with special needs and hiring a full-time learning specialist, ensuring that students were meeting the Archdiocesan Religion Guidelines and the California Curriculum Standards, having a credentialed full-time PE teacher and developing a solid plan for the future to continue attracting new families."

REVEREND WILLIAM AHLBACH

Father Bill Ahlbach, who grew up in the very shadow of St. Cecilia Church on 17th Avenue near Ulloa Street, was the eldest of six children born to Margaret and William Ahlbach, who were longtime St. Cecilia parishioners. With the encouragement of parish priests Father James Ward and Father John O'Day, Bill entered the diocesan high school seminary at the young age of thirteen and a half, just after he completed eighth grade at St. Cecilia

School in June 1950. He proceeded through four years of high school and then on to St. Patrick's Seminary for four years of college and, finally, four years of theology studies.

The seminary education in those days was both rigorous and almost medieval. Classes were taught in Latin, and Bill was allowed only one visit per month with his family. He was ordained at age twenty-five in June 1962 at St. Mary's Cathedral on Van Ness Avenue—the last group of priests ordained there just three months before it was destroyed by fire.

He was first assigned to St. Athanasius Parish in Mountain View and was later sent to Holy Name in San Francisco, St. Dunstan in Millbrae and St. Charles in San Carlos. In 1982, he was assigned to St. Matthew Parish in San Mateo, where he spent the last thirty-one years of his priestly ministry. He learned to say Mass in Spanish, organized a food locker for struggling families and was renowned for his booming voice and down-to-earth, engaging homilies. Parishioners remember his "walk a mile in Jesus' shoes" homily to First Communicants—he embellished it by taking off and waving his shoe over his head.

Fifty-one years after his ordination, Bill returned to his room at the St. Matthew Rectory following an evening Benediction service, when he was suddenly and unexpectedly called home by God. It is fitting that his last hour on earth was spent with Jesus in the Eucharist, whom he had given his life to serve. Bill was a big man with a big heart, loved his life as a priest and lived that vocation with generosity and grace.

Part of Father Ahlbach's legacy was the inspiration that he provided to his two youngest siblings, Mary and John, who followed his example by pursuing careers as Catholic educators: Mary teaching religious studies at St. Ignatius College Prep, where she has been since 1992, and her twin brother, John, teaching theology at Archbishop Riordan High School, where he has been since 1995.

Biography courtesy of Father Ahlbach's sister, Mary Ahlbach.

Sister Anne Dinneen (Sister Michele Denise), SNJM

Anne Kathleen Dinneen was born in San Francisco, California, on July 13, 1939, the first child of Jeremiah and Julia Dinneen, and along with her brother, Leo, she was raised in traditional Irish customs and very much a part of the Irish community in San Francisco. Anne found her parents' simple faith "an inspiration."

After graduating from St. Cecilia School, Mercy High School and College of the Holy Names, Anne was drawn by the friendliness of the SNJM Sisters and so entered the Sisters of the Holy Names novitiate in Los Gatos in 1958. As Sister Michele Denise, she professed her first vows there in 1960 and made her final vows on August 15, 1965.

After a few years in teaching assignments, Sister Anne entered a twenty-nine-year career in secondary education, noting, "I have found that teaching high school students is a much more rewarding and challenging experience than teaching at the junior high level."

It was during this time that Sister Anne appeared in several national magazines in an ad for Maytag washing machines! In an Irish tweed suit, she was pictured next to a Maytag commenting that the convent Maytag washer had survived many years of multiple daily loads.

In 1980, through her connection with CONCERN, an Irish organization committed to international development and relief, Sister Anne and her friend Sister Kate Ondreyco from Holy Names High School days participated in CONCERN's International Observer Program in the Honduran jungle for twenty-three days before being led to safety. Sister Anne and Sister Kate were especially attentive to the stories and needs of women.

After returning to an administrative post at Holy Names College for ten years, Sister Anne began to prepare for another ministry very dear to her heart, early childhood and parent education at a variety of preschools, including Head Start and Montessori, and working at St. Mary's Center Preschool, St. Vincent's Day Home in Oakland, Children's Village and St. Elizabeth/St. Joseph Special Education Needs Center in San Francisco.

During the last ten years of her life, Sister Anne experienced several health challenges that interrupted her ministry and involved lengthy recuperations. Each time she returned to health, she returned to active ministry—teaching preschool in Mississippi and ESL in Los Angeles and even sharing her knowledge of infant massage with Peruvian women via Skype.

Sister Anne entered eternal life on August 29, 2012. Her Mass of Resurrection was celebrated at Convent of the Holy Names, Los Gatos, California, with Father Michael Strange, SS, a friend and St. Cecilia classmate presiding.

Obituary from the website of the Sisters of the Holy Names of Jesus and Mary. Reprinted with permission.

St. Cecilia School Faculty Rosters, 1930–2016

With many thanks to School Principal Mrs. Marian Connelly and music teacher Sister Margaret Kinzie for their kind assistance in helping to compile these rosters.

School Year 1930–31

Gr. 1	Sister Veronica Maria
Gr. 2	Sister Miriam Elizabeth
Gr. 3	Sister Mary Eucharista
Gr. 4	Sister Mary Anthony
Gr. 5	Sister M. Loretta Rose
Gr. 6	Sister Bernard Mary
Gr. 7	n/a
Gr. 8	n/a

Principal: Sister Bernard Mary
Music teacher: Sister Frances Theresa

School Year 1931–32

Gr. 1	Sister Veronica Maria
Gr. 2	Sister Miriam Elizabeth
Gr. 3	Sister Mary Eucharista
Gr. 4	Sister Mary Anthony
Gr. 5	Sister M. Loretta Rose
Gr. 6	Sister Angela Clare

Gr. 7   Sister Bernard Mary
Gr. 8   n/a

Principal: Sister Bernard Mary
Music teacher: Sister Margaret Patricia

School Year 1932–33

Gr. 1   Sister Veronica Maria
Gr. 2   Sister Patrice Marie
Gr. 3   Sister Mary Eucharista
Gr. 4   Sister Mary Anthony
Gr. 5   Sister Frederick
Gr. 6   Sister M. Loretta Rose
Gr. 7   Sister Mary Scholastica
Gr. 8   Sister Bernard Mary

Principal: Sister Bernard Mary
Music teacher: Sister Bridget of Mary

School Year 1933–34

Gr. 1   Sister M. Agnes Gonzaga
Gr. 2   Sister M. Ann Christine
Gr. 3   Sister Mary Eucharista
Gr. 4   Sister Mary Anthony
Gr. 5   Sister M. Loretta Rose
Gr. 6   Sister Mary Melissa
Gr. 7   Sister Mary Scholastica
Gr. 8   Sister Mary Coronata

Principal: Sister Mary Coronata

School Year 1934–35

Gr. 1   Sister Mary Agnes Gonzaga
Gr. 2   Sister Mary Paraclita
Gr. 3   Sister Mary Eucharista
Gr. 4   Sister Mary Anthony
Gr. 5   Sister M. Loretta Rose
Gr. 6   Sister Mary Melissa

Gr. 7   Sister Mary Consuela
Gr. 8   Sister Mary Coronata

Principal: Sister Mary Coronata
Additional teachers: Sister Constance Mary

SCHOOL YEAR 1935–36

Gr. 1   Sister Mary Agnes Gonzaga
Gr. 2   Sister Virginia Mary
Gr. 3   Sister Mary Paraclita
Gr. 4   Sister Miriam Bernardine
Gr. 5   Sister Mary Anthony
Gr. 6   Sister Mary Melissa
Gr. 7   Sister Mary Consuela
Gr. 8   Sister Mary Coronata

Principal: Sister Mary Coronata
Additional teachers: Sister Constance Mary

SCHOOL YEAR 1936–37

Gr. 1   Sister Mary Agnes Gonzaga
Gr. 2   Sister Virginia Mary
Gr. 3   Sister Mary Paraclita
Gr. 4   Sister Constance Mary
Gr. 5   Sister Mary Anthony
Gr. 6   Sister Mary Melissa
Gr. 7   Sister Mary Consuela
Gr. 8   Sister Mary Coronata

Principal: Sister Mary Coronata

SCHOOL YEAR 1937–38

Gr. 1   Sister Mary Agnes Gonzaga
Gr. 2   Sister Mary Josephine
Gr. 3   Sister Virginia Mary
Gr. 4   Sister Constance Mary
Gr. 5   Sister Mary Paraclita
Gr. 6   Sister Mary Anthony

Gr. 7   Sister Mary Dara
Gr. 8   Sister Mary Coronata

Principal: Sister Mary Coronata
Music teacher: Sister Helen Dolores

SCHOOL YEAR 1938–39

Gr. 1   Sister Mary Agnes Gonzaga
Gr. 2   Sister Mary Josephine
Gr. 3   Sister Virginia Mary
Gr. 4   Sister Constance Mary
Gr. 5   Sister Mary Paraclita
Gr. 6   Sister Mary Anthony
Gr. 7   Sister Mary Dara
Gr. 8   Sister Mary Coronata

Principal: Sister Mary Coronata

SCHOOL YEAR 1939–40

Gr. 1   Sister Eileen Marie
Gr. 2   Sister Mary Josephine
Gr. 3   Sister Virginia Mary
Gr. 4   Sister Constance Mary
Gr. 5   Sister Mary Aquina
Gr. 6   Sister Antonia Marie
Gr. 7   Sister Mary Dara
Gr. 8   Sister Mary Emilita

Principal: Sister Mary Cecilia

SCHOOL YEAR 1940–41

Gr. 1   Sister M. Agatha Rose, Sister Eileen Marie
Gr. 2   Sister Teresa Maria
Gr. 3   Sister Mary Petra
Gr. 4   Sister Mary Josephine
Gr. 5   Sister Mary Karl
Gr. 6   Sister Mary Aquina
Gr. 7   Sister Mary Ambrosine
Gr. 8   Sister Mary Emilita

Appendix B

Principal: Sister Mary Cecilia

School Year 1941–42

Gr. 1	Sister Eileen Marie
Gr. 2	Sister Fidelia Maria
Gr. 3	Sister Mary Petra
Gr. 4	Sister Mary Amata
Gr. 5	Sister Mary Karl
Gr. 6	Sister M. Veronica Rose
Gr. 7	Sister Mary Scholastica
Gr. 8	Sister Mary Regina

Principal: Sister Mary Cecilia
Music teacher: Sister Theresa Rose

School Year 1942–43

Gr. 1	Sister M. Regina Rose
Gr. 2	Sister Fidelia Maria
Gr. 3	Sister Mary Petra
Gr. 4	Sister Mary Herbert
Gr. 5	Sister Mary Scholastica
Gr. 6	Sister Mary Vivian
Gr. 7	Sister Josephine Marie
Gr. 8	Sister Mary Consuela

Principal: Sister Mary Cecilia

School Year 1943–44

Gr. 1	Sister M. Agatha Rose
Gr. 2	Sister Gerarda Marie
Gr. 3	Sister Mary Benigna
Gr. 4	Sister Mary Petra
Gr. 5	Sister Mary Herbert
Gr. 6	Sister Mary Vivian
Gr. 7	Sister Mary Scholastica
Gr. 8	Sister Mary Consuela

Principal: Sister Mary Cecilia
Music teacher: Sister Mary Ignatia

SCHOOL YEAR 1944–45

Gr. 1   Sister M. Agatha Rose
Gr. 2   Sister Gerarda Marie
Gr. 3   Sister Mary Petra
Gr. 4   Sister Mary Benigna
Gr. 5   Sister Mary Vivian
Gr. 6   Sister Mary Raphaela
Gr. 7   Sister Mary Dara
Gr. 8   Sister Mary Lucina

Principal: Sister Mary Cecilia
Music teacher: Sister Bernard of Jesus

SCHOOL YEAR 1945–46

Gr. 1   Sister Marcelline Marie
Gr. 2   Sister Gerarda Marie
Gr. 3   Sister Mary Benigna
Gr. 4   Sister Mary Vivian
Gr. 5   Sister Mary Lucina
Gr. 6   Sister Mary Dara
Gr. 7   Sister Mary Raphaela
Gr. 8   Sister Miriam David

Principal: Sister Miriam David
Additional faculty: Sister Mary Dalora, Sister Paula Maria and Sister M. Rose Cecilia

SCHOOL YEAR 1946–47

Gr. 1   Sister Agatha Rose
Gr. 2   Sister Teresa Maria
Gr. 3   Sister Gerarda Marie
Gr. 4   Sister Bernadette Maria
Gr. 5   Sister Mary Lucina
Gr. 6   Mrs. Claire Strehl
Gr. 7   Sister Mary Raphaela
Gr. 8   Sister Miriam David

Principal: Sister Miriam David
Additional faculty: Sister Mary Bernadetta

SCHOOL YEAR 1947–48

Gr. 1   Sister Teresa Maria, Sister Mary of Nazareth
Gr. 2   Sister Gerarda Marie, Sister Thaddeus Mary
Gr. 3   Sister Eulalie Rose, Sister M. Louise Frances
Gr. 4   Miss Beverly Regan, Sister Mary Vivian
Gr. 5   Sister Bernadette Maria (Grades 4 and 5), Sister Mary Lucina
Gr. 6   Sister Mary Vivian, Mrs. Claire Strehl
Gr. 7   Miss Raney (Grades 6 and 7), Sister Mary Raphaela
Gr. 8   Sister Miriam David, Sister Mary Roberta

Principal: Sister Miriam David
Additional faculty: Sister M. Genevieve Agnes

SCHOOL YEAR 1948–49

K   Mrs. Mary J. Fitzpatrick
Gr. 1   Sister Thaddeus Mary, Sister Teresa Maria
Gr. 2   Sister Mary Eulalie Rose, Sister M. Louise Frances
Gr. 3   Sister Jeannette Marie, Sister Mary Christopher, Catherine Green
Gr. 4   Miss Beverly Regan, Sister Gerarda Marie
Gr. 5   Sister Mary Lucina, Miss Evelyn Lavelle
Gr. 6   Sister Mary Vivian, Sister Michaeline Mary
Gr. 7   Mrs. C. Miller, Sister Raphael Mary
Gr. 8   Sister Richard of Mary, Sister Miriam David

Principal: Sister Miriam David
Additional faculty: Sister Angela Louise and Sister Regina Maria

SCHOOL YEAR 1949–50

K   Mrs. Mary J. Fitzpatrick
Gr. 1   Sister Mary Anselma, Mrs. Patterson
Gr. 2   Sister Mary Thomasine, Sister Mary Eulalie Rose
Gr. 3   Sister Mary Christopher, Sister Beverly Regan
Gr. 4   Mrs. Viola G. McCauley, Sister Mary Ann Veronica
Gr. 5   Mrs. Virginia Burke, Sister Mary Christopher, Sister Gerarda Marie
Gr. 6   Sister Mary Vivian, Sister Mary Michael

Gr. 7   Sister Mary Scholastica, Sister Raphael Mary
Gr. 8   Sister Miriam David, Sister Mary Herbert

Principal: Sister Miriam David
Additional faculty: Sister Mary Carmela

School Year 1950–51

K   Mrs. Mary J. Fitzpatrick
Gr. 1   Sister Mary Anselma, Mrs. Patterson
Gr. 2   Sister Miriam Patrice, Sister Margaret Mary
Gr. 3   Sister Mary Bartholomew, Miss Beverly Regan
Gr. 4   Mrs. Marie K. Tobin, Sister M. Francis Paul
Gr. 5   Sister Miriam Thomas, Sister Mary Christopher
Gr. 6   Sister Mary Vivian, Sister Mary Michael
Gr. 7   Sister Mary Scholastica, Sister Raphael Mary
Gr. 8   Sister Mary Marina, Sister Mary Herbert

Principal: Sister Miriam David
Additional faculty: Sister Cornelia Mary, Sister M. Cecile Collette and Sister
   Mary Martha

School Year 1951–52

K   Mrs. Mary J. Fitzpatrick
Gr. 1   Sister Mary Anselma, Mrs. Patterson
Gr. 2   Sister Miriam Patrice, Sister Adele Mary
Gr. 3   Sister Mary Bartholomew, Sister Marion Timothy
Gr. 4   Mrs. Marie K. Tobin, Sister Johanna Mary, Sister Mary Scholastica
Gr. 5   Sister Loretta Maria, Sister Raphael Mary
Gr. 6   Sister Mary Vivian, Sister Mary Michael
Gr. 7   Sister Elise Marie, Sister Emilita, Sister Mary Scholastica
Gr. 8   Sister Michaeline Mary, Sister Mary Herbert

Principal: Sister Elise Marie
Additional faculty: Sister William Paul and Sister Cecile Collette

School Year 1952–53

K   Mrs. Mary J. Fitzpatrick
Gr. 1   Sister Mary Anselma, Sister M. Frances Rose

Gr. 2	Sister Adele Mary, Sister M. Florence Irene
Gr. 3	Alice Hanley, Sister Mary Bartholomew, Hazel Porter
Gr. 4	Mrs. Marie K. Tobin, Sister M. Eileen Theresa
Gr. 5	Sister Marion Timothy, Sister Loretta Maria
Gr. 6	Sister Mary Vivian, Sister Mary Michaeline
Gr. 7	Sister Mary Emilita, Sister Raphael Mary
Gr. 8	Sister Roberta Mary, Sister Cecile Collette

Principal: Sister Elise Marie

SCHOOL YEAR 1953–54

K	Mrs. Mary J. Fitzpatrick, Mrs. Scarpelli
Gr. 1	Sister Miriam Ann, Sister M. Frances Rose
Gr. 2	Sister Adele Mary, Sister M. Florence Irene
Gr. 3	Adelaide Egan, Sister Mary Bartholomew, Sister Miriam Mark
Gr. 4	Mrs. Marie K. Tobin, Sister M. Eileen Theresa
Gr. 5	Sister Marion Timothy, Sister Mary Vivian
Gr. 6	Mary Louise Naughton, Sister Mary Bartholomew, Sister Michaeline Mary
Gr. 7	Sister Mary Marcia, Sister Raphael Mary
Gr. 8	Sister Roberta Mary, Sister William Paul

Principal: Sister Elise Marie

SCHOOL YEAR 1954–55

K	Miss Louise Biancalana, Eugenia Sutton
Gr. 1	Sister Miriam Ann, Sister Miriam Eloise, Sister M. Dorothy Clare
Gr. 2	Sister M. Regina Clare, Sister M. Florence Irene
Gr. 3	Marguerite Ruiz, Sister M. Christine Dolora
Gr. 4	Mrs. Marie K. Tobin, Sister Magdalena Mary
Gr. 5	Sister Marion Patrick, Sister M. Catherine Elizabeth
Gr. 6	Sister Mary Consuela, Sister Mary Colman
Gr. 7	Sister Mary Marcia, Sister M. Eileen Catharine
Gr. 8	Sister Michaeline Mary, Sister Rose Genevieve

Principal: Sister M. Loretta Rose

Appendix B

School Year 1955–56

K	Miss Fitzpatrick
Gr. 1	Sister Therese Marian, Sister Miriam Eloise, Sister M. Dorothy Clare
Gr. 2	Sister M. Regina Clare, Sister M. Rita Margaret
Gr. 3	Alice Hanley, Sister M. Christine Dolora
Gr. 4	Mrs. Marie K. Tobin, Sister M. Carmela Rose
Gr. 5	Sister M. Joseph Paul, Sister M. Catherine Elizabeth
Gr. 6	Miss Patricia Pinnick, Sister Maureen Theresa
Gr. 7	Sister Mary Marcia, Sister M. Eileen Catharine
Gr. 8	Sister Michaeline Mary, Sister Rose Genevieve

Principal: Sister M. Loretta Rose

School Year 1956–57

K	Mercedes M. McAfee
Gr. 1	Sister Therese Marian, Sister Laurencie Marie
Gr. 2	Sister M. Elizabeth Bernadette, Sister M. Rita Margaret
Gr. 3	Mrs. Cecilia Brown, Sister M. Christine Dolora
Gr. 4	Mrs. Marie K. Tobin, Sister M. Carmela Rose
Gr. 5	Sister M. Joseph Paul, Sister Cordelia Maria
Gr. 6	Miss Patricia Pinnick, Sister Mary Scholastica
Gr. 7	Sister M. Amelia Clare, Sister M. Eileen Catharine
Gr. 8	Sister Michaeline Mary, Sister Eileen Marie

Principal: Sister M. Loretta Rose
Additional faculty: Sister William Paul

School Year 1957–58

Gr. 1	Sister Miriam George, Sister Laurencie Marie
Gr. 2	Sister M. Dorothy Clare, Sister M. Christine Dolora
Gr. 3	Mrs. Cecilia Brown, H. Fitzgerald
Gr. 4	Mrs. Marie K. Tobin, Sister Mary Theophane
Gr. 5	Sister M. Joseph Paul, Sister M. Elizabeth Bernadette
Gr. 6	Miss Patricia Pinnick, Sister Mary Scholastica
Gr. 7	Sister M. Charles Dominic, Sister M. Eileen Catharine
Gr. 8	Sister Mary Aloyse, Sister Francis Miriam

Appendix B

Principal: Sister Michaeline Mary
Additional faculty: Sister William Paul

School Year 1958–59

Gr. 1	Sister Miriam George, Sister Laurencie Marie
Gr. 2	Sister M. Dorothy Clare, Sister Rosanna Marie
Gr. 3	Mrs. Cecilia Brown, Mrs. Janigian
Gr. 4	Mrs. Marie K. Tobin, Sister Mary Theophane
Gr. 5	Sister M. Martin Christopher, Sister M. Patricia Rose
Gr. 6	Miss Patricia Pinnick, Sister M. Elizabeth Bernadette
Gr. 7	Sister M. Charles Dominic, Sister Mary Eucharista
Gr. 8	Sister M. Eileen Catharine, Sister Miriam Thomas

Principal: Sister Michaeline Mary
Additional faculty: Sister William Paul

School Year 1959–60

Gr. 1	Sister Miriam George, Sister Laurencie Marie
Gr. 2	Sister M. Dorothy Clare, Sister Rosanna Marie
Gr. 3	Mrs. Cecilia Brown, Mrs. Janigian
Gr. 4	Mrs. Marie K. Tobin, Sister Mary Theophane
Gr. 5	Sister M. Martin Christopher, Sister M. Patricia Rose
Gr. 6	Miss Patricia Pinnick, Sister M. Elizabeth Bernadette
Gr. 7	Sister M. Charles Dominic, Sister Mary Eucharista
Gr. 8	Sister M. Eileen Catharine, Sister Miriam Thomas

Principal: Sister Michaeline Mary
Additional faculty: Sister William Paul

School Year 1960–61

Gr. 1	Sister Joseph Miriam, Sister M. Virginia Therese
Gr. 2	Sister Mary Noella, Sister M. Joseph Anthony
Gr. 3	Sister Michael Marion, Mrs. JoAnn Todd
Gr. 4	Sister Ann Mary, Miss Bartol
Gr. 5	Mrs. Marie K. Tobin, Sister M. Patricia Rose
Gr. 6	Miss Patricia Pinnick, Sister Miriam Bernadine
Gr. 7	Sister Andrew Marie, Sister Mary Eucharista
Gr. 8	Sister M. Madeleine Rita, Sister Miriam Thomas

Appendix B

Principal: Sister Michaeline Mary
Additional faculty: Sister Guadalupe Maria

School Year 1961–62

Gr. 1	Sister Adrian Maria, Sister M. Virginia Therese
Gr. 2	Sister Mary Carmela, Sister M. Joseph Anthony
Gr. 3	Sister Michael Marion, Miss Dorothy Duffy
Gr. 4	Sister Ann Mary, Mrs. Midi Lampkin
Gr. 5	Mrs. Marie K. Tobin, Sister M. Patricia Rose
Gr. 6	Miss Patricia Pinnick, Sister Kenneth Marie
Gr. 7	Sister Andrew Marie, Sister Mary Eucharista
Gr. 8	Sister M. Madeleine Rita, Sister Maureen Theresa

Principal: Sister Michaeline Mary
Additional faculty: Sister Mary of the Sacred Heart

School Year 1962–63

Gr. 1	Sister Adrian Maria, Sister M. Rose Philomena
Gr. 2	Sister Ann Noel, Sister M. Joseph Anthony
Gr. 3	Miss Bridget Lawlor, Sister M. Patricia Agnes
Gr. 4	Sister Janice Mary, Miss Patricia Pinnick
Gr. 5	Mrs. Marie K. Tobin, Sister Mary Gertrudis
Gr. 6	Miss Rosemarie Gerber, Sister Kenneth Marie
Gr. 7	Sister Elizabeth Mary, Sister M. Cecile Collette
Gr. 8	Sister M. Madeleine Rita, Sister Maureen Theresa

Principal: Sister Mary of St. John
Additional faculty: Sister Mary of the Sacred Heart

School Year 1963–64

Gr. 1	Sister Adrian Maria, Sister Miriam Suzanne
Gr. 2	Mrs. Catherine Ring, Sister M. Helen Dolora, Sister M. Theresa Catherine
Gr. 3	Miss Judith Liberti, Sister Loretta Maria
Gr. 4	Sister M. Rose Philomena, Miss Patricia Pinnick
Gr. 5	Mrs. Marie K. Tobin, Sister Mary Gertrudis
Gr. 6	Miss Rosemarie Gerber, Sister Miriam Gertrude, Sister Janice Mary

Gr. 7   Sister Maria Anna, Sister Miriam Patrice
Gr. 8   Sister M. Madeleine Rita, Sister Maureen Theresa

Principal: Sister Mary of St. John
Additional faculty: Sister Bridget of Mary

School Year 1964–65

Gr. 1   Sister Adrian Maria, Sister Domenica Maria
Gr. 2   Sister Miriam Augusta, Sister M. Helen Dolora
Gr. 3   Mrs. Catherine Ring, Mrs. JoAnne Harding
Gr. 4   Sister Thaddeus Mary, Miss Patricia Pinnick
Gr. 5   Mrs. Marie K. Tobin, Sister Mary Gertrudis
Gr. 6   Sister M. Rose Philomena, Sister Miriam Gertrude
Gr. 7   Sister Maria Anna, Sister Miriam Patrice
Gr. 8   Sister M. Madeleine Rita, Sister Maureen Theresa

Principal: Sister Mary of St. John
Additional faculty: Sister Bridget of Mary

School Year 1965–66

Gr. 1   Sister Miriam Leo, Sister Domenica Maria
Gr. 2   Ann Sieh, Sister M. Kenneth Joseph
Gr. 3   Mrs. Catherine Ring, Sister Miriam Anita
Gr. 4   Sister Thaddeus Mary, Miss Patricia Pinnick
Gr. 5   Mrs. Marie K. Tobin, Sister Mary Cornelius
Gr. 6   Sister Miriam Gertrude, Miss Connie Lee
Gr. 7   Sister M. Elizabeth Bernadette, Sister Miriam Patrice
Gr. 8   Sister Maria Anna, Sister Maureen Theresa

Principal: Sister Mary of St. John
Additional faculty: Sister Bridget of Mary

School Year 1966–67

Gr. 1   Sister Joseph Miriam, Sister Terrence Marie
Gr. 2   Sister Miriam Anita, Mrs. Catherine Ring
Gr. 3   Miss Molloy, Mrs. O'Connor, Mrs. Flaherty
Gr. 4   Sister Thaddeus Mary, Miss Patricia Pinnick
Gr. 5   Mrs. Marie K. Tobin, Sister Mary Cornelius

Gr. 6   Sister Miriam Gertrude, Miss M. Sapinosa
Gr. 7   Sister M. Catherine Elizabeth, Sister Miriam Patrice
Gr. 8   Sister Mary Catherine Therese, Sister Maureen Theresa

Principal: Sister Mary of St. John
Additional faculty: Sister Marion Christopher

SCHOOL YEAR 1967–68

Gr. 1   Sister Kathleen Buzzard, Sister Mary Mannion
Gr. 2   Sister Terrence Marie, Mrs. Catherine Ring, Mrs. Flaherty
Gr. 3   Miss Molloy, Mrs. Jane Meuser, Mrs. Flaherty
Gr. 4   Sister Ann Mary, Miss Patricia Pinnick
Gr. 5   Miss Veronica McGrail, Sister Mary Cornelius
Gr. 6   Sister Miriam Gertrude, Mr. Thomas J. Kennedy
Gr. 7   Sister M. Eileen Catharine, Sister Sylvia Bartheld
Gr. 8   Sister Barbara Heinen, Sister Maureen Theresa

Principal: Sister Mary of St. John

SCHOOL YEAR 1968–69

Gr. 1   Sister Kathleen Buzzard, Sister Mary Mannion
Gr. 2   Sister Lorraine, Mrs. Mary Kae Fratini
Gr. 3   Mrs. Catherine Ring, Mrs. Lucene Thomason
Gr. 4   Sister Ann Mary, Miss Patricia Pinnick
Gr. 5   Sister Elizabeth Ann, Mr. T. McDonough
Gr. 6   Sister Miriam Gertrude, Mr. Arthur Cecchin
Gr. 7   Mr. Thomas J. Kennedy, Sister Elenora Marie
Gr. 8   Sister Dorothy Simpson, Sister Eileen Catharine

Principal: Sister Sylvia Bartheld

SCHOOL YEAR 1969–70

Gr. 1   Sister M. Agatha Rose, Sister Michelle Antonowicz
Gr. 2   Miss Georgene Glass, Mrs. Catherine Ring
Gr. 3   Mrs. Lucene Thomason, Mrs. Madeline Ward
Gr. 4   Sister M. Patricia Rose, Miss Patricia Pinnick
Gr. 5   Sister Elizabeth Ann Shields, Mr. T. McDonough
Gr. 6   Sister Miriam Gertrude, Miss Carmine Sing

Gr. 7   Mr. Arthur Cecchin, Sister Mary Hood
Gr. 8   Sister Dorothy Simpson, Sister M. Josepha Rose

Principal: Sister Sylvia Bartheld
Additional faculty: Sister Louise Bond

SCHOOL YEAR 1970–71

Gr. 1   Sister M. Agatha Rose, Sister Frances Pedersen
Gr. 2   Miss Georgene Glass, Mrs. Catherine Ring
Gr. 3   Mrs. Joan Baker, M. Gallo, Mrs. Janet Moran
Gr. 4   Miss Carmine Sing, Lucita Semmer, Mrs. Kathleen Wendt
Gr. 5   Miss Patricia Pinnick, Sister Eugenie Rohner
Gr. 6   Sister Bernice Breen, Sister Miriam Gertrude
Gr. 7   Mr. Arthur Cecchin, Sister Barbara Carroll
Gr. 8   Sister Stephanie Rose, Sister Louise Bond

Principal: Sister Sylvia Bartheld

SCHOOL YEAR 1971–72

Gr. 1   Sister M. Agatha Rose, Mrs. Maureen Mostyn-Brown
Gr. 2   Miss Carolyn Daley, Mrs. Catherine Ring
Gr. 3   Sister Teresa Maria, Mrs. Sheri Doran
Gr. 4   Miss Carmine Sing, Mrs. Kathleen Wendt
Gr. 5   Miss Patricia Pinnick, Mrs. Catherine Montano
Gr. 6   Sister Bernice Breen, Sister Miriam Gertrude
Gr. 7   Mr. Arthur Cecchin, Sister M. Helen Clare
Gr. 8   Sister Barbara Carroll, Sister Stephanie Rose

Principal: Sister Sylvia Bartheld

SCHOOL YEAR 1972–73

Gr. 1   Sister M. Agatha Rose, Mrs. Maureen Mostyn-Brown
Gr. 2   Miss Carolyn Daley, Mrs. Catherine Ring
Gr. 3   Mrs. Sheri Doran, Miss Nancy Cleveland, Sister Teresa Maria
Gr. 4   Miss Donna Addiego, Mrs. Kathleen Wendt
Gr. 5   Miss Patricia Pinnick, Mrs. Catherine Montano
Gr. 6   Miss Barbara Stimac, Sister Miriam Gertrude
Gr. 7   Mr. George Grandemange, Sister M. Helen Clare
Gr. 8   Sister Barbara Carroll, Mrs. Sheila Hood

Appendix B

Principal: Sister Sylvia Bartheld
Additional faculty: Sister M. Theresa Agnes

School Year 1973–74

Gr. 1   Sister M. Agatha Rose, Mrs. Maureen Mostyn-Brown
Gr. 2   Miss Carolyn Daley, Mrs. Catherine Ring
Gr. 3   Sister Dianne Fagan, Miss Nancy Cleveland
Gr. 4   Miss Donna Addiego, Mrs. Kathleen Wendt
Gr. 5   Miss Patricia Pinnick, Mrs. Catherine Montano
Gr. 6   Mrs. Barbara Stimac-Cecchin, Sister Miriam Gertrude
Gr. 7   Mr. George Grandemange, Sister M. Helen Clare
Gr. 8   Sister Miriam Donald, Mrs. Sheila Hood

Principal: Sister Sylvia Bartheld
Additional faculty: Sister M. Theresa Agnes

School Year 1974–75

Gr. 1   Sister M. Agatha Rose, Mrs. Maureen Mostyn-Brown
Gr. 2   Miss Carolyn Daley, Mrs. Catherine Ring
Gr. 3   Sister Dianne Fagan, Miss Nancy Cleveland
Gr. 4   Miss Donna Addiego, Mrs. Kathleen Wendt
Gr. 5   Miss Patricia Pinnick, Mrs. Catherine Montano
Gr. 6   Miss Patricia Jean Carson, Sister Miriam Gertrude
Gr. 7   Mr. George Grandemange, Sister M. Helen Clare
Gr. 8   Sister Miriam Donald, Mrs. Sheila Hood

Principal: Sister Adelemarie Dunne
Additional faculty: Sister M. Theresa Agnes

School Year 1975–76

Gr. 1   Sister M. Agatha Rose, Mrs. Maureen Mostyn-Brown
Gr. 2   Miss Carolyn Daley, Mrs. Catherine Ring
Gr. 3   Sister Mary Duffy, Miss Nancy Cleveland
Gr. 4   Miss Donna Addiego, Mrs. Kathleen Wendt
Gr. 5   Miss Patricia Pinnick, Mrs. Catherine Montano
Gr. 6   Miss Patricia Jean Carson, Sister Miriam Gertrude
Gr. 7   Mr. George Grandemange, Sister M. Helen Clare
Gr. 8   Sister Miriam Donald, Mrs. Sheila Hood

Appendix B

Principal: Sister Eleanore Maloney
Additional faculty: Sister M. Theresa Agnes

School Year 1976–77

Gr. 1	Miss Katherine Kays, Mrs. Maureen Mostyn-Brown
Gr. 2	Miss Carolyn Daley, Mrs. Catherine Ring
Gr. 3	Sister Mary Duffy, Miss Nancy Cleveland
Gr. 4	Miss Donna Addiego, Mrs. Betty Cavallero
Gr. 5	Miss Patricia Pinnick, Miss Jane Pesino
Gr. 6	Miss Patricia Jean Carson, Sister Miriam Gertrude
Gr. 7	Mr. John J. Donohue, Sister M. Helen Clare
Gr. 8	Sister Andrew Marie, Mrs. Sheila Hood

Principal: Sister Eleanore Maloney
Additional faculty: Sister M. Theresa Agnes

School Year 1977–78

Gr. 1	Miss Katherine Kays, Sister Marion Mills
Gr. 2	Miss Carolyn Daley, Mrs. Catherine Ring
Gr. 3	Ms. Enola Allen, Mrs. Theresa Watters
Gr. 4	Miss Donna Addiego, Mrs. Betty Cavallero
Gr. 5	Miss Patricia Pinnick, Miss Jane Pesino
Gr. 6	Sister Anita Forese, Sister Miriam Gertrude
Gr. 7	Miss Patricia Carson, Miss Deidre James
Gr. 8	Sister Marilyn Murphy, Mrs. Sheila Hood

Principal: Sister Eleanore Maloney
Additional faculty: Sister M. Theresa Agnes

School Year 1978–79

Gr. 1	Miss Katherine Kays, Ms. Enola Allen, Mrs. Kathleen Wendt
Gr. 2	Sister Margaret Kinzie, Mrs. Catherine Ring
Gr. 3	Miss Carolyn Daley, Mrs. Theresa Watters
Gr. 4	Miss Donna Addiego, Mrs. Betty Cavallero
Gr. 5	Mrs. Catherine Montano, Miss Jane Pesino
Gr. 6	Sister Anita Forese, Miss Patricia Pinnick
Gr. 7	Miss Patricia Carson, Mrs. M. Halpin, Mrs. Deidre Shannon
Gr. 8	Sister Marilyn Murphy, Mrs. Sheila Hood

Appendix B

Principal: Sister Eleanore Maloney
Additional faculty: Sister M. Theresa Agnes

School Year 1979–80

Gr. 1	Miss Katherine Kays, Miss Patricia Lyons
Gr. 2	Sister Margaret Kinzie, Mrs. Catherine Ring
Gr. 3	Miss Carolyn Daley, Mrs. Theresa Watters
Gr. 4	Miss Lourdes Grijalva, Miss Donna Addiego
Gr. 5	Mrs. Catherine Montano, Sister Therese Fenzl
Gr. 6	Miss Patricia Pinnick, Mrs. B. Alioto, Miss Frances Cavanagh
Gr. 7	Sister Mary Eileen, Miss Denise Malmquist, Mrs. Deidre Shannon
Gr. 8	Miss Margaret Barry, Mrs. Sheila Hood

Principal: Sister Marilyn Murphy

School Year 1980–81

K	Mrs. Lee Edgeman
Gr. 1	Mrs. Joan Leehane, Miss Patricia Lyons
Gr. 2	Sister Margaret Kinzie, Mrs. Catherine Ring
Gr. 3	Mrs. Carolyn Daley-Grimaud, Mrs. Theresa Watters
Gr. 4	Miss Lourdes Grijalva, Miss Donna Addiego
Gr. 5	Mrs. Catherine Montano, Sister Therese Fenzl
Gr. 6	Miss Patricia Pinnick, Miss Frances Cavanagh
Gr. 7	Miss Katherine Kays, Miss Denise Malmquist
Gr. 8	Mrs. Deidre Shannon, Mrs. Sheila Hood

Principal: Sister Marilyn Murphy
Additional faculty: Sister Francis Bernard Allen, Sister Helen Walsh and
  Sister Miriam Gertrude

School Year 1981–82

K	Mrs. Lee Edgeman
Gr. 1	Mrs. Joan Leehane, Miss Patricia Lyons
Gr. 2	Sister Margaret Kinzie, Mrs. Catherine Ring
Gr. 3	Mrs. Carolyn Grimaud, Mrs. Theresa Watters
Gr. 4	Miss Lourdes Grijalva, Miss Janice Arfsten
Gr. 5	Mrs. Catherine Montano, Sister Bernice Breen
Gr. 6	Miss Patricia Pinnick, Miss Frances Cavanagh

Gr. 7   Miss Katherine Kays, Miss Denise Malmquist
Gr. 8   Mrs. Deidre Shannon, Mrs. Sheila Hood

Principal: Sister Marilyn Murphy
Additional faculty: Sister Francis Bernard Allen, Sister Helen Walsh, Sister
    Miriam Gertrude and Sister Mary Theresa Agnes

SCHOOL YEAR 1982–83

K   Mrs. Lee Edgeman
Gr. 1   Mrs. Joan Leehane, Miss Patricia Lyons
Gr. 2   Sister Margaret Kinzie, Mrs. Catherine Ring
Gr. 3   Mrs. Carolyn Grimaud, Mrs. Theresa Watters
Gr. 4   Mrs. Catherine Montano, Miss Janice Arfsten
Gr. 5   Miss Claudine Aymard, Sister Bernice Breen
Gr. 6   Miss Patricia Pinnick, Miss Frances Cavanagh
Gr. 7   Mrs. Ina Potter, Miss Denise Malmquist
Gr. 8   Miss Katherine Kays, Mrs. Sheila Hood

Principal: Sister Marilyn Murphy
Additional faculty: Sister Helen Walsh, Sister Miriam Gertrude, Sister Mary
    Theresa Agnes and Sister Claire Duggan

SCHOOL YEAR 1983–84

K   Mrs. Lee Edgeman
Gr. 1   Mrs. Joan Leehane, Miss Patricia Lyons
Gr. 2   Sister Margaret Kinzie, Mrs. Catherine Ring
Gr. 3   Mrs. Carolyn Grimaud, Mrs. Theresa Watters
Gr. 4   Miss Frances Cavanagh, Miss Janice Arfsten
Gr. 5   Miss Claudine Aymard, Sister Bernice Breen
Gr. 6   Miss Patricia Pinnick, Miss Marian Mulkerrins
Gr. 7   Miss Mary McManus, Mrs. Denise Little
Gr. 8   Miss Katherine Kays, Mrs. Sheila Hood

Principal: Sister Marilyn Murphy
Additional faculty: Sister Helen Walsh, Sister Miriam Gertrude, Sister Mary
    Theresa Agnes and Sister Claire Duggan

Appendix B

K	Mrs. Lee Edgeman
Gr. 1	Mrs. Joan Leehane, Miss Patricia Lyons
Gr. 2	Sister Margaret Kinzie, Mrs. Catherine Ring
Gr. 3	Mrs. Carolyn Grimaud, Mrs. Theresa Watters
Gr. 4	Miss Frances Cavanagh, Miss Janice Arfsten
Gr. 5	Mrs. Claudine Hallisy, Sister Bernice Breen
Gr. 6	Miss Patricia Pinnick, Miss Marian Mulkerrins
Gr. 7	Miss Mary McManus, Mrs. Denise Little
Gr. 8	Miss Katherine Kays, Mrs. Sheila Hood

Principal: Sister Marilyn Murphy
Additional faculty: Sister Helen Walsh, Sister Miriam Gertrude, Sister Mary Theresa Agnes and Sister Claire Duggan

School Year 1985–86

K	Mrs. Lee Edgeman
Gr. 1	Mrs. Joan Leehane, Miss Patricia Lyons
Gr. 2	Sister Margaret Kinzie, Mrs. Catherine Ring
Gr. 3	Mrs. Carolyn Grimaud, Mrs. Theresa Watters
Gr. 4	Miss Frances Cavanagh, Miss Janice Arfsten
Gr. 5	Mrs. Claudine Hallisy, Sister Bernice Breen
Gr. 6	Miss Patricia Pinnick, Miss Marian Mulkerrins
Gr. 7	Miss Mary McManus, Mrs. Denise Little
Gr. 8	Miss Katherine Kays, Mrs. Sheila Hood

Principal: Sister Marilyn Murphy
Additional faculty: Sister Helen Walsh, Sister Miriam Gertrude, Sister Mary Theresa Agnes, Sister Claire Duggan and Sister Kathryn Trenary

School Year 1986–87

K	Mrs. Theresa Watters, Miss Marie Lindemann
Gr. 1	Mrs. Joan Leehane, Miss Patricia Lyons
Gr. 2	Sister Margaret Kinzie, Mrs. Catherine Ring
Gr. 3	Mrs. Carolyn Grimaud, Mrs. Claudine Hallisy
Gr. 4	Miss Frances Cavanagh, Miss Janice Arfsten
Gr. 5	Mrs. Yvonne Benedict, Sister Bernice Breen
Gr. 6	Miss Patricia Pinnick, Miss Marian Mulkerrins

Gr. 7   Miss Mary McManus, Mrs. Denise Little
Gr. 8   Miss Katherine Kays, Mrs. Sheila Hood

Principal: Sister Marilyn Murphy
Additional faculty: Sister Helen Walsh, Sister Miriam Gertrude, Sister Mary
     Theresa Agnes, Sister Claire Duggan and Sister Kathryn Trenary

SCHOOL YEAR 1987–88

K   Mrs. Theresa Watters, Miss Marie Lindemann
Gr. 1   Mrs. Joan Leehane, Miss Patricia Lyons
Gr. 2   Sister Margaret Kinzie, Mrs. Catherine Ring
Gr. 3   Miss Carolyn Daley, Mrs. Claudine Hallisy
Gr. 4   Miss Frances Cavanagh, Miss Janice Arfsten
Gr. 5   Mrs. Yvonne Benedict, Sister Bernice Breen
Gr. 6   Miss Patricia Pinnick, Miss Marian Mulkerrins
Gr. 7   Miss Mary McManus, Mrs. Denise Malmquist-LIttle
Gr. 8   Miss Katherine Kays, Mrs. Sheila Hood

Principal: Sister Marilyn Murphy
Additional faculty: Sister Helen Walsh, Sister Miriam Gertrude, Sister Mary
     Theresa Agnes, Sister Claire Duggan and Sister Kathryn Trenary

SCHOOL YEAR 1988–89

K   Mrs. Theresa Watters, Miss Marie Lindemann
Gr. 1   Mrs. Joan Leehane, Miss Patricia Lyons
Gr. 2   Sister Margaret Kinzie, Mrs. Catherine Ring
Gr. 3   Miss Carolyn Daley, Miss Patricia Pinnick
Gr. 4   Miss Frances Cavanagh, Miss Janice Arfsten
Gr. 5   Mrs. Yvonne Benedict, Sister Bernice Breen
Gr. 6   Miss Monica Ambrosi, Miss Marian Mulkerrins
Gr. 7   Miss Mary McManus, Mrs. Denise Little
Gr. 8   Miss Katherine Kays, Mrs. Sheila Hood

Principal: Sister Marilyn Murphy
Additional faculty: Sister Helen Walsh, Sister Miriam Gertrude, Sister Mary
     Theresa Agnes, Sister Claire Duggan and Sister Kathryn Trenary

SCHOOL YEAR 1989–90

K   Mrs. Theresa Watters, Miss Marie Lindemann
Gr. 1   Mrs. Joan Leehane, Miss Patricia Lyons

Gr. 2   Sister Margaret Kinzie, Mrs. Catherine Ring
Gr. 3   Miss Carolyn Daley, Miss Patricia Pinnick
Gr. 4   Miss Frances Cavanagh, Miss Janice Arfsten
Gr. 5   Mr. David Ristuccia, Sister Bernice Breen
Gr. 6   Miss Bernadette O'Sullivan, Miss Marian Mulkerrins
Gr. 7   Miss Mary McManus, Mrs. Denise Little
Gr. 8   Miss Katherine Kays, Mrs. Sheila Hood

Principal: Sister Marilyn Murphy
Additional faculty: Sister Helen Walsh, Sister Miriam Gertrude, Sister Mary Theresa Agnes, Sister Claire Duggan, Sister Kathryn Trenary and Sister Eleanore Maloney

SCHOOL YEAR 1990–91

K   Mrs. Theresa Watters, Miss Marie Lindemann
Gr. 1   Mrs. Joan Leehane, Mr. Daniel Halton
Gr. 2   Sister Margaret Kinzie, Mrs. Catherine Ring
Gr. 3   Miss Carolyn Daley, Miss Patricia Pinnick
Gr. 4   Miss Frances Cavanagh, Miss Janice Arfsten
Gr. 5   Miss Patricia Lyons, Mrs. Marie McNier
Gr. 6   Ms. Lynne P. Morris, Mrs. Marian Connelly
Gr. 7   Mr. Gene Ide, Mrs. Denise Little
Gr. 8   Miss Katherine Kays, Mrs. Sheila Hood

Principal: Sister Marilyn Murphy
Additional faculty: Sister Helen Walsh, Sister Miriam Gertrude, Sister Kathryn Trenary, Sister Claire Duggan and Sister Ann Gilchrist

SCHOOL YEAR 1991–92

K   Mrs. Theresa Watters, Miss Marie Lindemann
Gr. 1   Mrs. Joan Leehane, Ms. Mary Radanovich
Gr. 2   Sister Margaret Kinzie, Mrs. Catherine Ring
Gr. 3   Miss Carolyn Daley, Miss Patricia Pinnick
Gr. 4   Miss Frances Cavanagh, Miss Janice Arfsten
Gr. 5   Miss Patricia Lyons, Sister Bernice Breen
Gr. 6   Ms. Lynne P. Morris, Mrs. Marian Connelly
Gr. 7   Mr. David Ristuccia, Mrs. Denise Little
Gr. 8   Miss Katherine Kays, Mr. Eugene Ide

Principal: Sister Marilyn Murphy

Additional faculty: Sister Helen Walsh, Sister Miriam Gertrude, Mrs. Mary Greene, Mrs. Noreen McNamara, Mrs. Mary McKeon, Mrs. Sandy Koch, Mrs. Ann Brown, Sister Ann Gilchrist, Miss Mary McManus and Ms. Lydia Krivoy

Several Sisters have served at St. Cecilia School during nonconsecutive periods. Some of them are:

Sister Mary Eucharista:
1930–1936 and 1958–1962

Sister Miriam Patrice (later, Sister Colleen Kern):
1950–52 and 1963–67

Sister M. Eileen Catharine (later, Sister Kathleen McDonough)
1954–1960 and 1967–69

Sister M. Catherine Elizabeth
1954–1956 and 1968–74 (as Sister Sylvia Bartheld)

Sister Andrew Marie:
1959–62 and 1979–91 (as Sister Marilyn Murphy)

Sister Mary of St. John:
1962–68 as principal and 1982–91 (as Sister Claire Duggan) as supplemental program teacher

Sister Eleanore Maloney:
1975–79 as principal and 1989–90 as supplemental program teacher

SCHOOL YEAR 1992–93

K	Mrs. Teri Watters, Mrs. Eileen Donohoe
Gr. 1	Mrs. Joan Leehane, Ms. Mary Radanovich
Gr. 2	Sister Margaret Kinzie, Mrs. Catherine Ring
Gr. 3	Miss Carolyn Daley, Miss Patricia Pinnick
Gr. 4	Miss Frances Cavanagh, Miss Janice Arfsten

Gr. 5   Miss Patricia Lyons, Sister Bernice Breen
Gr. 6   Mrs. Christine Gonzalez, Mrs. Marian Connelly
Gr. 7   Mrs. Margaret Elsbernd, Mrs. Denise Malmquist-Little
Gr. 8   Miss Katherine Kays, Mrs. Sheila Hood

Principal: Sister Marilyn Miller
Additional faculty: Mrs. Marie McDonnell Murphy and Mr. Gene Ide

SCHOOL YEAR 1993–94

K   Mrs. Teri Watters, Mrs. Eileen Donohoe
Gr. 1   Mrs. Joan Leehane, Ms. Mary Radanovich
Gr. 2   Sister Margaret Kinzie, Mrs. Catherine Ring
Gr. 3   Miss Carolyn Daley, Miss Patricia Pinnick
Gr. 4   Miss Frances Cavanagh, Miss Janice Arfsten
Gr. 5   Miss Patricia Lyons, Sister Bernice Breen
Gr. 6   Mrs. Christine Gonzalez, Mrs. Marian Connelly
Gr. 7   Mrs. Margaret Elsbernd, Mrs. Denise Malmquist-Little
Gr. 8   Miss Katherine Kays, Mrs. Sheila Hood

Principal: Sister Marilyn Miller
Additional faculty: Mrs. Marie McDonnell Murphy and Mr. Gene Ide

SCHOOL YEAR 1994–95

K   Mrs. Teri Watters, Mrs. Eileen Donohoe
Gr. 1   Mrs. Joan Leehane, Ms. Mary Radanovich
Gr. 2   Sister Margaret Kinzie, Mrs. Catherine Ring
Gr. 3   Miss Carolyn Daley, Miss Patricia Pinnick
Gr. 4   Miss Frances Cavanagh, Miss Janice Arfsten
Gr. 5   Miss Patricia Lyons, Sister Bernice Breen
Gr. 6   Mrs. Christine Gonzalez, Mrs. Marian Connelly
Gr. 7   Mrs. Margaret Elsbernd, Mrs. Denise Malmquist-Little
Gr. 8   Miss Katherine Kays, Mr. Gene Ide

Principal: Sister Marilyn Miller
Additional faculty: Mrs. Marie McDonnell Murphy and Sister Catherine Nessi

SCHOOL YEAR 1995–96

K   Mrs. Teri Watters, Mrs. Eileen Donohoe
Gr. 1   Mrs. Joan Leehane, Ms. Mary Radanovich

Gr. 2   Sister Margaret Kinzie, Mrs. Catherine Ring
Gr. 3   Miss Carolyn Daley, Miss Patricia Pinnick
Gr. 4   Miss Frances Cavanagh, Miss Janice Arfsten
Gr. 5   Miss Laurie Herberg Wofford, Sister Bernice Breen
Gr. 6   Mrs. Christine Gonzalez, Mrs. Marian Connelly
Gr. 7   Mrs. Margaret Elsbernd, Mrs. Denise Malmquist-Little
Gr. 8   Miss Katherine Kays, Mr. Gene Ide

Principal: Sister Marilyn Miller
Additional faculty: Mrs. Marie McDonnell Murphy and Sister Catherine Nessi

SCHOOL YEAR 1996–97

K   Mrs. Teri Watters, Mrs. Eileen Donohoe
Gr. 1   Mrs. Joan Leehane, Ms. Mary Radanovich
Gr. 2   Sister Margaret Kinzie, Mrs. Nancy Brightman
Gr. 3   Miss Carolyn Daley, Miss Patricia Pinnick
Gr. 4   Miss Frances Cavanagh, Miss Janice Arfsten
Gr. 5   Miss Laurie Herberg Wofford, Sister Bernice Breen
Gr. 6   Mrs. Christine Gonzalez, Mrs. Marian Connelly
Gr. 7   Mrs. Margaret Elsbernd, Mrs. Denise Malmquist-Little
Gr. 8   Miss Katherine Kays, Mr. Gene Ide

Principal: Sister Marilyn Miller
Additional faculty: Mrs. Marie McDonnell Murphy and Sister Catherine Nessi

SCHOOL YEAR 1997–98

K   Mrs. Teri Watters, Mrs. Eileen Donohoe
Gr. 1   Miss Anne Bray, Ms. Mary Radanovich
Gr. 2   Sister Margaret Kinzie, Mrs. Nancy Brightman
Gr. 3   Miss Carolyn Daley, Miss Patricia Pinnick
Gr. 4   Miss Frances Cavanagh, Miss Janice Arfsten
Gr. 5   Miss Laurie Herberg Wofford, Sister Bernice Breen
Gr. 6   Mrs. Christine Gonzalez, Mrs. Marian Connelly
Gr. 7   Mrs. Margaret Elsbernd, Mrs. Denise Malmquist-Little
Gr. 8   Miss Katherine Kays, Mr. Gene Ide

Principal: Sister Marilyn Miller
Additional faculty: Mrs. Marie McDonnell Murphy and Sister Catherine Nessi,

SCHOOL YEAR 1998–99

K	Mrs. Teri Watters, Mrs. Eileen Donohoe
Gr. 1	Miss Anne Bray, Ms. Mary Radanovich
Gr. 2	Sister Margaret Kinzie, Mrs. Nancy Brightman
Gr. 3	Miss Carolyn Daley, Miss Patricia Pinnick
Gr. 4	Miss Frances Cavanagh, Miss Janice Arfsten
Gr. 5	Miss Laurie Herberg Wofford, Sister Bernice Breen
Gr. 6	Mrs. Christine Gonzalez, Mrs. Marian Connelly
Gr. 7	Mrs. Margaret Elsbernd, Mrs. Denise Malmquist-Little
Gr. 8	Miss Katherine Kays, Mrs. Marie McDonnell Murphy

Principal: Sister Marilyn Miller
Additional faculty: Mrs. Peggy O'Donnell Sister Catherine Nessi and Mr. Gene Ide

SCHOOL YEAR 1999–2000

K	Mrs. Teri Watters, Mrs. Eileen Donohoe
Gr. 1	Miss Anne Bray, Ms. Mary Radanovich
Gr. 2	Sister Margaret Kinzie, Mrs. Sue Dudley
Gr. 3	Miss Carolyn Daley, Miss Patricia Pinnick
Gr. 4	Miss Frances Cavanagh, Miss Janice Arfsten
Gr. 5	Mr. Darin Fong, Mrs. Kate Downing Ortega
Gr. 6	Mrs. Christine Gonzalez, Mrs. Marian Connelly
Gr. 7	Mrs. Margaret Elsbernd, Mrs. Denise Malmquist-Little
Gr. 8	Miss Katherine Kays, Mrs. Marie McDonnell Murphy

Principal: Sister Marilyn Miller
Additional faculty: Mrs. Peggy O'Donnell, Sister Catherine Nessi and Mr. Gene Ide

SCHOOL YEAR 2000–2001

K	Mrs. Teri Watters, Mrs. Eileen Donohoe
Gr. 1	Miss Anne Bray, Ms. Mary Radanovich
Gr. 2	Sister Margaret Kinzie, Mrs. Elizabeth Ostadan
Gr. 3	Miss Carolyn Daley, Miss Patricia Pinnick
Gr. 4	Miss Frances Cavanagh, Miss Janice Arfsten
Gr. 5	Mr. Darin Fong, Mrs. Kate Downing Ortega
Gr. 6	Mrs. Christine Gonzalez, Mrs. Marian Connelly

Gr. 7   Mrs. Margaret Elsbernd, Mrs. Denise Malmquist-Little
Gr. 8   Miss Katherine Kays, Mrs. Marie McDonnell Murphy

Principal: Sister Marilyn Miller
Additional faculty: Mrs. Peggy O'Donnell, Sister Catherine Nessi and Mr. Gene Ide

School Year 2001–2

K   Mrs. Teri Watters, Mrs. Eileen Donohoe
Gr. 1   Miss Anne Bray, Ms. Mary Radanovich
Gr. 2   Sister Margaret Kinzie, Mrs. Elizabeth Ostadan
Gr. 3   Miss Carolyn Daley, Miss Patricia Pinnick
Gr. 4   Miss Frances Cavanagh, Miss Janice Arfsten
Gr. 5   Mr. Darin Fong, Mrs. Kate Downing Ortega
Gr. 6   Mrs. Christine Gonzalez, Mrs. Marian Connelly
Gr. 7   Mrs. Margaret Elsbernd, Mrs. Denise Malmquist-Little
Gr. 8   Miss Katherine Kays, Mrs. Marie McDonnell Murphy

Principal: Sister Marilyn Miller
Additional faculty: Mrs. Peggy O'Donnell, Sister Catherine Nessi and Mr. Gene Ide

School Year 2002–3

K   Mrs. Teri Watters, Mrs. Eileen Donohoe
Gr. 1   Mrs. Sue Holland, Ms. Mary Radanovich
Gr. 2   Sister Margaret Kinzie, Mrs. Elizabeth Ostadan
Gr. 3   Miss Carolyn Daley, Miss Patricia Pinnick
Gr. 4   Miss Christine Reeder, Miss Janice Arfsten
Gr. 5   Mr. Darin Fong, Mrs. Kate Downing Ortega
Gr. 6   Mrs. Christine Gonzalez, Mrs. Marian Connelly
Gr. 7   Mrs. Margaret Elsbernd, Mrs. Denise Malmquist-Little
Gr. 8   Miss Katherine Kays, Mrs. Marie McDonnell Murphy

Principal: Sister Marilyn Miller
Additional faculty: Mrs. Peggy O'Donnell, Sister Catherine Nessi and Mr. Gene Ide

School Year 2003–4

K   Mrs. Teri Watters, Mrs. Eileen Donohoe
Gr. 1   Mrs. Sue Holland, Ms. Mary Radanovich

Gr. 2   Sister Margaret Kinzie, Mrs. Elizabeth Ostadan
Gr. 3   Miss Carolyn Daley, Miss Patricia Pinnick
Gr. 4   Miss Christine Reeder, Miss Janice Arfsten
Gr. 5   Mr. Darin Fong, Mrs. Kate Downing Ortega
Gr. 6   Mrs. Christine Gonzalez, Mrs. Marian Connelly
Gr. 7   Mrs. Sheila Truesdell, Mrs. Denise Malmquist-Little
Gr. 8   Miss Katherine Kays, Mrs. Marie McDonnell Murphy

Principal: Sister Marilyn Miller
Additional faculty: Mrs. Peggy O'Donnell, Sister Catherine Nessi and Mr. Gene Ide

SCHOOL YEAR 2004–5

K   Mrs. Teri Watters, Mrs. Eileen Donohoe
Gr. 1   Mrs. Sue Holland, Ms. Mary Radanovich ·
Gr. 2   Sister Margaret Kinzie, Mrs. Sharon Brown Shea
Gr. 3   Miss Carolyn Daley, Miss Patricia Pinnick
Gr. 4   Miss Christine Reeder, Miss Janice Arfsten
Gr. 5   Mr. Darin Fong, Mrs. Kate Downing Ortega
Gr. 6   Mrs. Christine Gonzalez, Mrs. Marian Connelly
Gr. 7   Mrs. Sheila Truesdell, Mrs. Denise Malmquist-Little
Gr. 8   Miss Katherine Kays, Mrs. Marie McDonnell Murphy

Principal: Sister Marilyn Miller
Additional faculty: Mrs. Peggy O'Donnell, Sister Catherine Nessi and Mr. Gene Ide

SCHOOL YEAR 2005–6

K   Mrs. Teri Watters, Mrs. Eileen Donohoe
Gr. 1   Mrs. Sue Holland, Ms. Mary Radanovich
Gr. 2   Sister Margaret Kinzie, Mrs. Sharon Brown Shea
Gr. 3   Miss Carolyn Daley, Mrs. Sue Courey
Gr. 4   Mrs. Marguerite Rodigou, Miss Janice Arfsten
Gr. 5   Mr. Darin Fong, Mrs. Kate Downing Ortega
Gr. 6   Mrs. Christine Gonzalez, Mrs. Marian Connelly
Gr. 7   Mrs. Sheila Truesdell, Mrs. Denise Malmquist-Little
Gr. 8   Miss Katherine Kays, Mrs. Marie McDonnell Murphy

Principal: Sister Marilyn Miller
Additional faculty: Mr. Adam Vincent, Sister Catherine Nessi and Mr. Gene Ide

Appendix B

School Year 2006–7

K	Mrs. Teri Watters, Mrs. Eileen Donohoe
Gr. 1	Mrs. Sue Holland, Ms. Mary Radanovich
Gr. 2	Sister Margaret Kinzie, Mrs. Sharon Brown Shea
Gr. 3	Miss Carolyn Daley, Ms. Deborah Denehy
Gr. 4	Mrs. Alison Porto Holthouser, Miss Stephanie Santy
Gr. 5	Mr. Darin Fong, Mrs. Kate Downing Ortega
Gr. 6	Mrs. Christine Gonzalez, Mrs. Marian Connelly
Gr. 7	Mrs. Sheila Truesdell, Mrs. Denise Malmquist-Little
Gr. 8	Miss Katherine Kays, Mrs. Marie McDonnell Murphy

Principal: Sister Marilyn Miller
Additional faculty: Mr. Adam Vincent, Sister Catherine Nessi and Mr. Gene Ide

School Year 2007–8

K	Mrs. Teri Watters, Mrs. Eileen Donohoe
Gr. 1	Mrs. Sue Holland, Ms. Mary Radanovich
Gr. 2	Sister Margaret Kinzie, Mrs. Sharon Brown Shea
Gr. 3	Miss Carolyn Daley, Ms. Deborah Denehy
Gr. 4	Mrs. Alison Porto Holthouser, Miss Stephanie Santy
Gr. 5	Mr. Darin Fong, Mr. Christopher Watters
Gr. 6	Mrs. Christine Gonzalez, Mrs. Marian Connelly
Gr. 7	Mrs. Sheila Truesdell, Mrs. Denise Malmquist-Little
Gr. 8	Miss Katherine Kays, Mrs. Marie McDonnell Murphy

Principal: Sister Marilyn Miller
Additional faculty: Mr. Adam Vincent, Sister Catherine Nessi and Mr. Gene Ide

School Year 2008–9

K	Mrs. Teri Watters, Mrs. Eileen Donohoe
Gr. 1	Mrs. Sue Holland, Ms. Mary Radanovich
Gr. 2	Sister Margaret Kinzie, Mrs. Sharon Brown Shea
Gr. 3	Miss Carolyn Daley, Ms. Deborah Denehy
Gr. 4	Mrs. Alison Porto Holthouser, Miss Stephanie Santy
Gr. 5	Mr. Darin Fong, Mr. Christopher Watters
Gr. 6	Mrs. Christine Gonzalez, Mrs. Marian Connelly
Gr. 7	Mrs. Sheila Truesdell, Mrs. Denise Malmquist-Little
Gr. 8	Miss Katherine Kays, Mrs. Beth Tunney Fergus

Appendix B

Principal: Sister Marilyn Miller
Additional faculty: Mr. Adam Vincent, Sister Catherine Nessi and Mr. Gene Ide

School Year 2009–10

K	Mrs. Teri Watters, Mrs. Eileen Donohoe
Gr. 1	Mrs. Sue Holland, Ms. Mary Radanovich
Gr. 2	Sister Margaret Kinzie, Mrs. Sharon Brown Shea
Gr. 3	Miss Carolyn Daley, Ms. Deborah Denehy
Gr. 4	Mrs. Alison Porto Holthouser, Miss Stephanie Santy
Gr. 5	Mr. Darin Fong, Mr. Christopher Watters
Gr. 6	Mrs. Christine Gonzalez, Mrs. Marian Connelly
Gr. 7	Mrs. Sheila Truesdell, Mrs. Denise Malmquist-Little
Gr. 8	Miss Katherine Kays, Mrs. Beth Tunney Fergus

Principal: Sister Marilyn Miller
Additional faculty: Mr. Adam Vincent, Sister Catherine Nessi and Mr. Gene Ide

School Year 2010–11

K	Mrs. Teri Watters, Mrs. Eileen Donohoe
Gr. 1	Mrs. Sue Holland, Ms. Mary Radanovich
Gr. 2	Sister Margaret Kinzie, Mrs. Sharon Brown Shea
Gr. 3	Miss Carolyn Daley, Ms. Deborah Denehy
Gr. 4	Mrs. Alison Porto Holthouser, Miss Stephanie Santy
Gr. 5	Mr. Darin Fong, Mr. Christopher Watters
Gr. 6	Mrs. Christine Gonzalez, Mrs. Marian Connelly
Gr. 7	Mrs. Sheila Truesdell, Mrs. Denise Malmquist-Little
Gr. 8	Miss Katherine Kays, Mrs. Beth Tunney Fergus

Principal: Sister Marilyn Miller
Additional faculty: Mr. Adam Vincent, Sister Catherine Nessi and Mr. Gene Ide

School Year 2011–12

K	Mrs. Teri Watters, Mrs. Eileen Donohoe
Gr. 1	Mrs. Sue Holland, Ms. Mary Radanovich
Gr. 2	Sister Margaret Kinzie, Mrs. Sharon Brown Shea
Gr. 3	Miss Carolyn Daley, Ms. Deborah Denehy
Gr. 4	Mrs. Alison Porto Holthouser, Miss Stephanie Santy

Gr. 5	Mr. Darin Fong, Mr. Christopher Watters
Gr. 6	Mrs. Christine Gonzalez, Mrs. Marian Connelly
Gr. 7	Mrs. Sheila Truesdell, Ms. Anne Sculley
Gr. 8	Miss Katherine Kays, Mrs. Beth Tunney Fergus

Principal: Sister Marilyn Miller
Additional faculty: Mr. Adam Vincent, Sister Catherine Nessi and Mr. Gene Ide

SCHOOL YEAR 2012–13

K	Mrs. Teri Watters, Mrs. Eileen Donohoe
Gr. 1	Mrs. Sue Holland, Ms. Mary Radanovich
Gr. 2	Sister Margaret Kinzie, Mrs. Sharon Brown Shea
Gr. 3	Mrs. Maureen Cassidy Faherty, Ms. Deborah Denehy
Gr. 4	Mrs. Alison Porto Holthouser, Miss Stephanie Santy
Gr. 5	Mr. Darin Fong, Ms. Katherine Dzida
Gr. 6	Mrs. Christine Gonzalez, Mrs. Rose Sullivan Stewart
Gr. 7	Mrs. Sheila Truesdell, Ms. Anne Sculley
Gr. 8	Miss Katherine Kays, Mrs. Beth Tunney Fergus

Principal: Mrs. Marian Connelly
Assistant Principal: Mr. Adam Vincent
Additional faculty: Mr. Christopher Watters and Mr. Gene Ide

SCHOOL YEAR 2013–14

K	Mrs. Teri Watters, Mrs. Eileen Donohoe
Gr. 1	Mrs. Sue Holland, Ms. Mary Radanovich
Gr. 2	Sister Margaret Kinzie, Mrs. Sharon Brown Shea
Gr. 3	Mrs. Maureen Cassidy Faherty, Ms. Deborah Denehy
Gr. 4	Mrs. Alison Porto Holthouser, Miss Stephanie Santy
Gr. 5	Mr. Darin Fong, Ms. Katherine Dzida
Gr. 6	Mrs. Christine Gonzalez, Mrs. Rose Sullivan Stewart
Gr. 7	Mrs. Sheila Truesdell, Ms. Anne Sculley
Gr. 8	Miss Katherine Kays, Mrs. Beth Tunney Fergus

Principal: Mrs. Marian Connelly
Assistant Principal: Mr. Adam Vincent
Additional faculty: Mr. Christopher Watters and Mr. Gene Ide

Appendix B

K	Mrs. Teri Watters, Mrs. Eileen Donohoe
Gr. 1	Mrs. Sue Holland, Ms. Mary Radanovich
Gr. 2	Miss Christina Balistreri, Mrs. Sharon Brown Shea
Gr. 3	Mrs. Rossana DeFillipo, Ms. Deborah Denehy
Gr. 4	Mrs. Maureen Cassidy Faherty, Miss Stephanie Santy
Gr. 5	Mr. Darin Fong, Ms. Katherine Dzida
Gr. 6	Mrs. Eileen Woods, Mr. Jarrod Formalejo
Gr. 7	Mrs. Rose Sullivan Stewart, Ms. Anne Sculley
Gr. 8	Miss Katherine Kays, Mrs. Beth Tunney Fergus

Principal: Mrs. Marian Connelly

Assistant Principal: Mr. Adam Vincent

Additional faculty: Mr. Christopher Watters, Mr. Gene Ide and Sister Margaret Kinzie

School Year 2015–16

K	Mrs. Teri Watters, Mrs. Eileen Donohoe
Gr. 1	Mrs. Sue Holland, Ms. Mary Radanovich
Gr. 2	Miss Christina Balistreri, Mrs. Sharon Brown Shea
Gr. 3	Mrs. Rossana DeFillipo, Ms. Deborah Denehy
Gr. 4	Mrs. Maureen Cassidy Faherty, Miss Stephanie Santy
Gr. 5	Mr. Darin Fong, Ms. Katherine Dzida
Gr. 6	Mrs. Eileen Woods, Mr. Jarrod Formalejo
Gr. 7	Mrs. Rose Sullivan Stewart, Ms. Anne Sculley
Gr. 8	Miss Katherine Kays, Mrs. Beth Tunney Fergus

Principal: Mrs. Marian Connelly

Assistant Principal: Mrs. Emily Murphy

Additional faculty: Mr. Christopher Watters, Mr. Gene Ide and Sister Margaret Kinzie

About the Author

Frank Dunnigan was born at St. Mary's Hospital in San Francisco and baptized in the old St. Cecilia Church on 17th Avenue in January 1952. He graduated from St. Cecilia School (class of 1966), from St. Ignatius College Prep (class of 1970) and then from the University of San Francisco. After a career in both banking and retail, he is a recent retiree after nearly twenty years of service with the federal government and is living in suburban Phoenix, Arizona.

He is the author of *Growing Up in San Francisco's Western Neighborhoods: Boomer Memories from Kezar Stadium to Zim's Hamburgers*, published by The History Press (2014), as well as *Growing Up in San Francisco: More Boomer Memories from Playland to Candlestick Park*, also published by The History Press (2016).

Since January 2009, he has written "Streetwise," a monthly column on local history published by Western Neighborhoods Project (www.outsidelands.org). He has also contributed text and photo content to the published works of other local historians.

The author has donated all royalties from the initial two-thousand-copy printing of this book to St. Cecilia Parish to benefit the Monsignor Collins School Fund.